B-17 FLYING FORTRESS UNITS

OF THE PACIFIC WAR

SERIES EDITOR: TONY HOLMES

OSPREY COMBAT AIRCRAFT • 39

B-17 FLYING FORTRESS UNITS

OF THE PACIFIC WAR

Martin Bowman

PUBLISHING

Front cover
At 0800 hrs on the morning of 5 January 1943, six B-17F Flying Fortresses from the 43rd Bombardment Group (BG) and a similar number of B-24D Liberators from the 90th BG lumbered into the sky from Port Moresby's Seven-Mile strip and Ward's Drome and headed north, bound for the Japanese stronghold of Rabaul. Leading the formation was the Commander of Fifth Bomber Command, Brig Gen Kenneth N Walker. Technically, he should not have been on this mission, as his boss, Fifth Air Force Commander Maj Gen George C Kenney, had banned him from further flights over enemy territory in October 1942. This mission on Rabaul was an important one, however, as Allied reconnaissance flights had detected 21 warships and 300,000 tons of merchant shipping concentrated in Rabaul Harbour.

A veteran of 35 years of service in the Army Air Corps, and one of a select cadre of officers whose creativity, dedication and fearlessness had prepared the USAAF for combat during the inter-war years, Walker had helped formulate the basic strategic bombing plan that would guide his air force throughout World War 2. Posted from the 5th BG in Hawaii to the Allied Air Forces in Australia in June 1942, Walker had flown 16 missions from northern Australia and New Guinea by early 1943, much to the consternation of Maj Gen Kenney. Having helped plan the attack on Rabaul Harbour, Brig Gen Walker now wanted to play an active part in the mission itself.

Heading the formation of bombers across the formidable Owen Stanley Range towards Rabaul was B-17F 41-24458 *San Antonio Rose* of the 64th BS/43rd BG. Aside from its regular nine-man crew, headed by squadron CO Maj Allen Lindberg, the aircraft also included 43rd BG Deputy CO Maj Jack Bleasdale and Brig Gen Kenneth Walker. Arriving over the target area in bright sunshine at noon, the B-17s and B-24s proceeded to drop their bombs on vessels in the harbour from a height of 9000 ft. As the formation turned for home, *San Antonio Rose* continued to circle the target area whilst Brig-Gen Walker took photos of the area with his new camera. The bomber was then hit by flak, the

First published in Great Britain in 2003 by Osprey Publishing
Elms Court, Chapel Way, Botley, Oxford, OX2 9LP

ISBN 1 84176 481 7

Edited by Tony Holmes and Neil Maxwell
Page design by Tony Truscott
Cover Artwork by Mark Postlethwaite
Aircraft Profiles and Scale Drawings by Mark Styling
Index by Alan Thatcher
Origination by Grasmere Digital Imaging, Leeds
Printed in China through Bookbuilders

03 04 05 06 07   10 9 8 7 6 5 4 3 2 1

EDITOR'S NOTE
To make this best-selling series as authoritative as possible, the Editor would be interested in hearing from any individual who may have relevant photographs, documentation or first-hand experiences relating to the world's elite pilots, and their aircraft, of the various theatres of war. Any material used will be credited to its original source. Please write to Tony Holmes at 10 Prospect Road, Sevenoaks, Kent, TN13 3UA, Great Britain, or by e-mail at:
tony.holmes@osprey-jets.freeserve.co.uk

ACKNOWLEDGEMENTS
The Author would like to thank the following individuals for their assistance:
Mike Bailey, Bernice 'Bernie' Barr, Grp Capt Antony Barwood OBE, RAF Retd, Steve Birdsall, Boeing, Michael Claringbould (www.aerothentic.com), the late William M Cleveland, the late Alfred B Cohen, Jim Dieffenderfer, Douglas Aircraft, Ken Fields, Roger A Freeman, Frederick A Johnsen, Frank P Hohmann, John H Mitchell, Janice Olsen and Ken Wright of *B-17 Combat Crewmen and Wingmen*, Graham Simons of GMS and Glen Spieth.

B-17 being seen to fall behind the remaining USAAF aircraft, smoke trailing from one engine. Moments later Japanese Ki-43-I 'Oscars' (from the 11th *Sentai*) and A6M3 Zeros (from the 252nd, 253rd and 582nd *Kokutai*) attacked the bombers, three of them latching onto the already smoking *San Antonio Rose*. Badly shot up, the B-17 was eventually lost from sight some 20 miles south of Rabaul. No American crewmen saw the aircraft crash, and despite an extensive search of the area, no survivors were found.

As the third-most senior officer in the Fifth Air Force, Brig Gen Kenneth Walker proved to be the highest-ranking USAAF officer lost in combat during World War 2. On the recommendation of Gen Douglas MacArthur, Supreme Commander of the South-west Pacific Area, Walker was subsequently awarded a posthumous Medal of Honor (*Cover artwork by Mark Postlethwaite*)

CONTENTS

TO THE BRINK OF WAR

On 2 July 1941 the United States Army Air Forces (USAAF) came into being under the command of Maj Gen Henry 'Hap' Arnold. That same month, President Franklin D Roosevelt asked the Secretaries of War and of the Navy to produce estimates for bringing their forces to an effective war footing. Arnold used this opportunity to gain permission for the USAAF's Air War Plans Division (AWPD) to prepare its own report, forcing the War Plans Division to concentrate solely on the needs of its land forces. Arnold's staff officers at AWPD, headed by Col Harold L George, and including Lt Col Kenneth N Walker, Maj Haywood 'Possum' Hansell and Maj Larry S Kuter, formulated a policy (AWPD/1) of a relentless air offensive against Germany and a strategic defence in the Pacific. If Japan entered the war, it too would be subjected to aerial bombardment after Germany had surrendered.

America placed great faith in a new four-engined bomber which had achieved legendary status on screen and in the press – the Boeing Flying Fortress. Hollywood movies like *Test Pilot* had in 1938 featured the early Y1B-17 version of the 'wonder bomber', while Col Robert C Olds' 2nd Bombardment Group (BG) set transcontinental and long-distance records. In reality, in 1939 there were barely 13 operational Y1B-17s, and orders for only 39 follow-up B-17Bs, which, like the Y1B-17, were poorly armed.

B-17B 35-211 MD105 (assigned to the Air Corps' Material Division at Wright Field on 2 August 1939, hence the 'MD' unit designator) is seen in flight. The first of 39 B-models to be built by Boeing, this aircraft was used for armament testing at Wright Field. It was eventually written off on 2 December 1943. The aircraft commander's offset blister behind the cockpit was duly moved to the centreline on the B-17D (*Boeing*)

Daylight operations by the Royal Air Force's No 90 Sqn in Europe with the Fortress I (B-17C) in 1941 soon revealed armament deficiencies and operational weaknesses, and the accuracy of the Norden and Sperry precision bombsights in combat conditions was questionable.

Cpl Frank P Hohmann was with the 74th Attack Squadron, 6th Attack Group (AG) at Rio Hato, in Panama, in 1941. The unit had Northrop A-24s and two B-17Bs on strength. He recalls;

'We knew the Norden bombsight couldn't do what the brass said it would do – put a bomb in a pickle barrel from 20,000 ft. When the Army Air Force trained a group of navigators to operate the equipment in order prove the brass right, the test results were made top secret when the bombs dropped a mile from the target! I had just passed the exam to train as a pilot, but I turned down flight training in favour of becoming a flight engineer for Capt Jay P Rousek, who had come into the unit from B-17B flight training, and was a graduate of West Point.

'All of a sudden a new job was handed to me – learn the top turret. But they forgot to order ammo for the guns! The Model 299 had rolled out of the factory on 16 July 1935. It had no top gun position. The B-17C had no top gun turret either, but the builders did look at the 0.30-cal gun that was mounted in the nose and made the big change when building the next model, the B-17D. It was also decided that the engines needed cowling flaps, but no gun for the flight engineer, so the moral of this story is that I never had gunner's training.

'I don't know how the other flight engineers learned. I learned to operate the turret by tracking birds walking on the beaches wherever we were. While in Panama "Uncle Sam" did get us some Enfield rifles to learn to carry. They had no ammo either. I was given a Colt 0.45 and had to buy six rounds at six cents each to feel what that gun felt like to fire. I was given an expert medal for firing that many rounds!'

During the first week of December 1941 eight more B-17Bs and 19 B-18s were delivered to the 6th AG to defend the Panama Canal.

By mid-1941, the misplaced confidence shown in the B-17 helped persuade the War Department that the Philippines could be defended, and they 'would not only be defended but reinforced'.

Secretary of War Henry L Stimpson maintained that a force of B-17s could form a cost-effective deterrent to Japanese aggression in the region, and a means by which the Philippines might become a 'self-sustaining fortress capable of blockading the China Sea by air power'. Washington also hoped that if America should go to war with Japan, then the Soviet Union would allow US bombers to shuttle between Luzon's Clark Field, near Manila, and Vladivostok, attacking the Japanese home islands en route.

Deliveries of the much-improved B-17D models began on 3 February 1941. Some were earmarked for the Philippines, where they would join the newly created US Army Forces in the Far East, commanded by Gen Douglas MacArthur, who was recalled to active duty in July 1941. His air element, the Air Forces, US Army Forces in the Far East (constituted as the Philippine Department Air Force on 16 August 1941 and activated on 20 September), was commanded by Brig Gen Henry B Clagett, and had only 100 pilots and 40 obsolete aircraft. Early that year the thinking in Washington was that if Japan

invaded, troops in the Philippines would 'hold out as long as they could on their own'.

With a ferry range of more than 2000 miles, the B-17D could be flown directly to the Philippines. This was less of a risk than sending the aircraft by sea through the Japanese Bonin group or the Carolines, Palaus, Marshalls and Marianas – the former German colonies entrusted to Japan after World War 1.

On 21 May 1941, 21 B-17C/Ds of the 19th BG, commanded by Col Eugene L Eubank, flew from Hamilton Field, California, to Hickam Field, Hawaii. Some months later, on 5 September, a composite squadron of nine B-17Ds from the 5th and 11th BGs of the Hawaiian Air Force (later redesignated the Seventh Air Force), led by Maj (later Gen) Emmett 'Rosie' O'Donnell Jr, took off on the first leg of their journey to the Philippines.

The 14th BS staged through Midway, Wake, Port Moresby and Darwin, in Australia. The Wake Island-Port Moresby leg crossed the Japanese-controlled Caroline Islands, so the crews maintained radio silence, flying at night at 26,000 ft – an altitude believed to be beyond the reach of Japanese fighters. Bad weather on the final leg between Darwin and Clark Field failed to deter the crews, and they landed at Clark in driving rain on 12 September.

Two newly built B-17Ds are seen on the Boeing ramp in Seattle on 5 February 1941. The first D-model was not handed over to the USAAC until the early spring of that year. The B-17D incorporated many design changes as a result of the experience gained in combat by the RAF in Europe *(Boeing)*

B-17Ds of the 19th BG overfly the main gate at Hickam Field, Hawaii, in May 1941. Some 21 B-17C/Ds had been flown out to Hawaii on the 21st of that month *(via Bill Cleveland)*

Meanwhile, to avoid further flights over the Japanese-controlled islands, a South Pacific route was devised from Hawaii to Christmas Island, Canton Island, Nandi, in the Fiji group, Noumea, on New Caledonia, and Townsville, in Australia.

On 28 October 1941, the Air Forces, US Army Forces in the Far East became the Far East Air Force (FEAF) under the command of Maj Gen Lewis H Brereton. On the same day V Bomber Command was constituted, but it had only one heavy bombardment group, the 19th. At the end of November another 26 B-17Cs and Ds, led by Lt Col Eubank, joined the 14th BS at Clark Field. To defend the Philippines, Brereton had, by 1 December, about 100 Curtiss P-40s and 68 obsolete Seversky P-35As and Boeing P-26As spread between six airfields. A radar site at Iba Field fed information by telephone and telegraph to an interceptor command at nearby Nielson Field.

By moving the B-17s from Clark Field to a grass strip at Del Monte – a small satellite field on the island of Mindanao, some 600 miles to the south – the aircraft could be put beyond the range of Japanese fighters operating from Formosa (Taiwan). The plan was that if the Japanese invaded, the US crews could stage through Clark Field to attack an invasion fleet.

Meanwhile, plans were advanced to send more B-17s to the Philippines. On 6 December, Maj Gen Arnold visited Hamilton Field, where two flights of B-17s, led by Majs R H Carmichael and T H Landon, were preparing to head to the Philippines. Relations between the US and Japan had deteriorated since the last trans-Pacific flight, causing concern for the safety of the Fortresses as they passed over the Carolines. Arnold said 'I assembled the officers and told them they would probably run into trouble somewhere along the line'.

Trouble would come much earlier in the journey than any of them had expected. At 0755 hrs on Sunday 7 December 1941, the Pearl Harbor naval base at Oahu, in the Hawaiian Islands, was attacked by 190 carrier-borne aircraft from a Japanese strike force. America knew that Japan was preparing for war, but had expected that the first bombs would fall on the Philippines or Malaya.

Two trainee radar operators on a rudimentary mobile set north of Pearl Harbor reported the large formation, but the Hawaiian base commander assumed the aircraft were some expected B-17s and the radar operators were told to stand down. Mitsubishi A6M Zero-Sen or Type 0 fighters roared over the island at low level, machine-gunning B-17s, P-40s, Catalinas and other aircraft parked in neat rows at Wheeler Field and Kaneohe. Among the units on the ground at Hickam was the 11th BG, which comprised the 14th, 26th and 42nd BSs, as well as the 50th Reconnaissance Squadron (RS).

Horst Handrow, an air gunner in the 50th RS who had emigrated with his family from Germany as a child in 1932, was in his barracks;

B-17E 41-2443, which was assigned to the 42nd BS/11th BG at Hickam on 15 December 1941, was lost off Hawaii with Lt Cox's crew on 5 April 1942. Note the power-operated Bendix gun turret. The ventral bathtub was deleted on the first 112 B-17Es and replaced with a solid Bendix power-operated gun turret with twin 0.50-cals fired by a gunner lying prone and facing aft, sighting the guns through a periscope arrangement of angled mirrors. The turret proved troublesome to operate and was subsequently replaced with the much improved Sperry ball turret with the gunner squeezed inside. A second Sperry turret – an A-1 electrically-operated dorsal turret with twin 0.50-cals – was installed behind the cockpit just in front of the radio room, the latter still carrying the normal 0.50-cal machine gun. Ammunition feed was from six 125-round boxes mounted below the guns, using disintegrating link belts. As with previous variants, the single 0.30-cal in the nose was retained, as it was thought that no enemy fighter pilots would attempt a head-on attack with such high closing speeds between fighter and bomber (*Boeing*)

'I was just getting out of bed and looking for my Sunday paper which hadn't come yet. Cursing to myself a little, I thought I'd take it out on Lester, my buddy, and so I started to beat him on the head with my pillow. The fight was on when an explosion rocked the barracks. Lester fell and I hit the floor. Now what in the hell could have caused that! Lester was dead – I could see a three-inch hole in his neck. Then another explosion. I ran to the window, and with the roar of a dive-bomber overhead, I saw this aeroplane dive, aeroplane and all, right into HAD (HQ Air Division). The HAD seemed to leave the ground and then settle again in a blast of burning metal and wood.

'The red circle on the next aeroplane's wing gave out the story. We were at war. I grabbed a machine gun and rushed out to my aeroplane, "81". Then I ran back for another. When I got back, some Jap had shot the tail off! Next time, the aeroplane went up into the air and settled back a burning mass of metal. We lost all our aeroplanes the same way. About 12 Zeros strafed the parking ramp with incendiary fire and set almost all the B-17s and B-18s on fire.'

Four of the 11th BG's six B-17Ds were destroyed. At Pearl Harbor, torpedo-bombers and dive-bombers attacked the 86 ships of the American Pacific Fleet at anchor, inflicting heavy casualties. Eight battleships were reduced to heaps of twisted, blazing metal. The USS *Arizona* was hit in the forward magazine by a bomb which had pierced several decks, the vessel exploding in a pall of smoke and flame. She sank with more than a thousand men still inside. Within about 25 minutes seven other battleships had been either destroyed or severely

Capt Raymond Swenson's 38th RS B-17C 40-2070 was caught on approach to Hickam Field by strafing Japanese fighters, who left it burned out on the tarmac. The bomber's flare storage box had been struck by rounds fired by the Japanese fighters as the Fortress approached Hickam. The pilot managed to land the burning B-17, which broke in half upon hitting the ground and came to rest just short of the Hale Makai barracks. All but one of the aircraft's crew survived this harrowing ordeal (*USAF*)

Wrecked B-17C/Ds of the 11th BG lay scattered on the tarmac at Hickam Field after the Japanese attack on 7 December 1941. B-18s and B-17s of the 50th RS (centre right) appear to have survived the surprise raid unscathed (*USAF*)

damaged, left listing in the water. Five of the 12 B-17Ds of the 5th BG, lined up in neat rows at Hickam, were also destroyed.

Twelve B-17Ds of the 7th BG (two of the original 14 had turned back early in the flight from Hamilton Field) and four B-17Cs and two B-17Es of the 88th BS/7th BG, all of which were en route to the Philippines, arrived over Hawaii during the Japanese attack. They had no ammunition so that more fuel could be carried, and to compensate for the additional fuel stored aft of the centre of gravity, the armour had been removed from the crew positions and placed, along with the guns, forward in the fuselage.

The pilots hastily landed wherever they could. Lt Frank Bostrom put down on a golf course, while some, like Maj Richard H Carmichael and Lt Robert Richards, landed on the small fighter strip at Bellows Field (Richards and his crew were all subsequently killed during a mission to Rendova Island on 8 September 1942). Lt Brandon and his crew, including navigator 'Bunky' Snider, jumped from their Fortress before the wheels had finished turning, sheltering in a drainage ditch as strafing Japanese fighters destroyed their B-17.

Fortunately, not all the 7th BG B-17s flew to Hawaii on this fateful day, as Lt John W Fields, a co-pilot/navigator in the 22nd BS, recalls:

'We were to pick up new B-17Es – the first ones to come off the production line – from the Sacramento Air Depot. As soon as we had got our aeroplanes we were to report to Hamilton Field and were to have left on the night of 6 December. We were picking up our aeroplanes one at a time, and there were various things wrong with them, minor things, so we didn't all get them on the same day.'

Boeing had received orders for 812 B-17Es, which became a more combat-worthy version of the Fortress in the wake of the experience gained by the RAF's No 90 Sqn in Europe.

Material shortages delayed production, and the first B-17E did not make its maiden flight until 5 September 1941. The E-model had greatly enlarged tail surfaces for better control and stability for high-altitude bombing, and the rear fuselage from the radio compartment on was redesigned to provide more space for the gunners. The tail was extended six feet to include a 'stinger' gun position, boasting two 0.50-cal Browning M2 machine guns fired by the gunner in an uncomfortable half-kneeling, half-sitting position on a bicycle-type seat.

Instead of leaving for Hickam Field on the night of 6 December, Lt John Fields flew a 'shake-down' flight with Capt Bill Lewis, the squadron operations officer and deputy commander. Lewis was an

ex-airline pilot who had been called back into the Air Corps on active duty. The first that Fields knew of the attack on Pearl Harbor was when he was woken up on 7 December at about 1100 hrs by his squadron commander, Maj Kenneth B Hobson. Fields continues;

'He said, "Pearl Harbor's been attacked. We've got to get our aeroplanes off and take them to Muroc Lake". We all immediately began to get our stuff packed and out to the aeroplanes. I flew as co-pilot with Maj Hobson, with a crew chief. We didn't have a navigator or any gunners. I was squadron armaments officer, and they immediately told us to take our bomb-bay tanks out and load the ship with bombs because they were fearful that a Japanese fleet was steaming towards the West Coast, and that they were going to move in on the West Coast and take it.

'We dropped our bomb-bay tanks and loaded up with bombs, then they changed their orders again and we took the bombs out and put the bomb-bay tanks back in. This went on for about seven days, and during all this time we were out chasing imaginary fleets up and down the West Coast, flying out of Muroc.'

Fields finally left Hamilton Field on 16 December, when ten Fortresses set out for Hickam;

'The runways had been cleared off, but many buildings had been bombed, and there were burned aircraft visible along the side of the runways. There was still smoke from burning vessels in Pearl Harbor and an oil slick all over the water. It was really a mess. On a visit there I was shocked to see the number of capsized and burned boats in the harbor and in the dry docks. I saw the battleships *Utah*, *California*, *Arizona*, *West Virginia* and the *Oklahoma*, as well as several destroyers, either burned or in some other way totally disabled. In some of the ships I learned that many bodies were still unrecovered.

'There was a 20 mm aircraft gun emplacement just outside the officers' barracks at Hickam where I stayed, and the gunners told me that it was five days before they got any ammunition for their gun, so they felt pretty low. They were just not equipped for an attack on Pearl Harbor or Hickam Field.

Six Fortresses en route from California arrived in Hawaiian skies in the midst of the Japanese attack on Pearl Harbor. Immediately set upon by Zeros, the B-17 pilots landed wherever they could. Lt Robert Richards of the 38th RS/19th BG bellied B-17C 40-2049 in at Bellows Field, a fighter strip at Kahuhu, 40 miles from Hickam, while under attack from Japanese fighters' strike on the Hawaiian Islands on 7 December 1941. The Fortress was landed downwind, and it wrecked a P-40 before coming to rest and being strafed by enemy aircraft. Two crewmembers were wounded (*USAF*)

B-17Ds burn fiercely at Hickam Field shortly after the Japanese attacks on 7 December 1941 (*USAF*)

'The Hawaiian Department countermanded our orders, which had been to go to "Plum" (Mindanao), impounded our equipment and put us to work flying patrol missions for the *Lexington* force out of Hawaii. Finally, and largely through Maj Hobson's insistence, they decided to let three crews go – Hobson, J R Dubose and Jack Hughes. They departed for Mindanao but they never got there, although they did make it to Java, where they met the 19th BG which had evacuated from the Philippines.'

Twenty-nine B-17Es of the 7th BG were hurriedly diverted to Muroc to help defend California from possible Japanese attack. Only 19 B-17Bs could be sent to Spokane, Washington, to join the five B-17Cs of the 19th BG that were already there, while a paltry two B-17Bs were stationed in Alaska. Six B-17Bs (and one B-18) of the 41st RS were based in Newfoundland. In the weeks following the Japanese attack, 46 B-17s were sent to reinforce the Hawaiian Islands, where 18 were retained as a strike force to attack any further Japanese task force.

In the Philippines, Gen MacArthur's HQ knew within an hour that Pearl Harbor had been bombed, the news reaching the FEAF via commercial radio on Luzon between 0300-0330 hrs local time.

However, the FEAF units were mostly caught on the ground, just as the units at Hawaii had been. Within 30 minutes of the news reaching MacArthur's forces, the radar at Iba Field picked up a formation of aircraft 75 miles offshore, heading for Corregidor, an island at the entrance to Manila Bay. P-40s were ordered to intercept but failed to make contact. Shortly before 0930 hrs aircraft were detected over Lingayen Gulf, heading towards Manila.

What orders were issued next are lost in the fog of confusion. Gen Brereton was to insist later that he recommended to MacArthur's headquarters that to prevent them being caught on the ground the 18 B-17s at Clark Field should be used in an immediate strike on Japanese airfields on Formosa. MacArthur and his Chief of Staff, Maj Gen Richard K Sutherland, denied that any such request was made. Sutherland argued that the B-17s should have been at Del Monte, on Mindanao, beyond the range of the Japanese bombers. MacArthur claimed that an attack on Formosa would be suicidal.

However, it seems that a raid on Formosa was proposed but the mission was postponed to permit a last-minute reconnaissance of the target to be carried out. Lt Col Eugene Eubank did not receive orders for a photo-reconnaissance mission until mid-morning on 8 December and by then it was too late.

Early morning fog on Formosa prevented the majority of Japanese Army aircraft from taking off to bomb targets around Lingayen Gulf,

75 miles north of Clark Field, while the 100+ Navy bombers scheduled to leave at 0700 hrs remained grounded until 1000 hrs. However, at about 0800 hrs, probably in reaction to those Japanese Army bombers which had managed to take off and which were heading for Lingayen Gulf, the two squadrons of B-17s were ordered aloft and told to remain up until the enemy had left. While they were airborne, orders were received to bomb Formosa with or without a photo-reconnaissance, and the first Fortresses began landing at Clark Field at around 1100 hrs to refuel and load bombs.

Unfortunately, P-40s which had been sent into the air earlier also landed at Clark and Iba for refuelling, and by 1130 hrs radar revealed a second Japanese formation 70 miles west of Lingayen Gulf, heading south. The information centre at Nielson Field realised that Clark was among the targets, and issued a warning – it arrived too late to save either the fighters or the bombers.

At about 1145 hrs fighters were ordered off from Del Carmen to patrol Clark Field, but they failed to arrive before two waves of Japanese aircraft attacked shortly after noon. The P-40s were preparing to take off, while 17 Fortresses (another was airborne on reconnaissance) were still being loaded up. They were caught cold. All the aircraft except three P-40s, which took off and tangled with the enemy bombers, were destroyed in strafing attacks. Apart from the sole B-17 which was airborne, all that now remained of the Fortress force in-theatre were 17 B-17Cs of the 14th BS at Del Monte. During the morning and afternoon of 9 December, the 19th BG mounted a limited reconnaissance mission in search of the Japanese invasion force, the bombers then landing at Clark and at San Marcelino (between Clark and Del Monte).

The next day five B-17Cs mounted the first US bombing raid of the war when they attacked a Japanese convoy landing troops and equipment at Vigan and Aparri, in northern Luzon. Maj 'Rosie' O'Donnell, 14th BS CO,

B-17D 40-3095 of the 19th BG fell into the hands of the Japanese after being strafed on the ground at Clark Field on 8 December 1941 and abandoned by retreating US forces. It was rebuilt by the Japanese using parts from other wrecked aircraft and accompanied a second D-model and a B-17E, both similarly rebuilt, to Japan for evaluation (*USAF*)

The captured early-build B-17E is seen in flight from B-17D 40-3095. Altogether, the Japanese obtained three Fortresses (two B-17Ds and one early B-17E) which were flown to Japan and put on public display with other captured US aircraft. These Fortresses were carefully evaluated and then used by the Japanese to develop fighter tactics to counter the US heavy bombers. The Japanese considered the B-17 a tough and well-armed adversary, and one that was very difficult to shoot down. It could absorb an incredible amount of damage and still remain airborne (*USAF*)

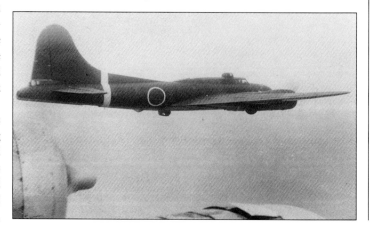

made five runs over his targets before his bombs would release, while Capt Elmer L Parsel's crew claimed a hit on a transport. Three other 14th BS crews dropped 100-lb bombs on transports at Vigan or on targets of opportunity at Aparri. There had only been time to load one 600-lb bomb aboard Lt G R Montgomery's B-17 and this was dropped on the Japanese transports. Montgomery returned to Clark for another bomb-load, and this time he was armed with 20 'hundred pounders'. Attacking the target area alone, he was forced to ditch four miles off Del Monte, but all the crew were rescued.

Lt George E Schaetzel's B-17, carrying eight 600-lb bombs, was attacked by Zeros and badly hit. Schaetzel managed to lose the fighters in cloud and landed the badly damaged Fortress at San Marcelino with one engine out.

The third B-17C, piloted by Capt Colin P Kelly Jr, carried only three 600-lb bombs. Kelly ignored the Japanese landing operations underway at Vigan and carried on to Aparri in search of an enemy aircraft carrier which had been reported in the area. Finding no sign of the vessel, Kelly returned to Vigan and attacked the heavy cruiser *Ashigara* from 22,000 ft. One of the three bombs dropped by bombardier Cpl Meyer Levin was thought to have hit the aft gun turret and set the ship alight.

A group of Zeros then chased the B-17 and caught up with it about 50 miles from Clark Field. Successive attacks destroyed parts of the aircraft, and fire broke out in the bomb-bay. Waist gunner Sgt Delhany was decapitated by a burst of machine gun fire and Pte Altman was wounded. Kelly bravely fought to keep the Fortress straight and level while his co-pilot, Lt Donald Robbins, and four other crew baled out. Despite being fired on by the circling Zeros, they all landed safely at Clark, but the B-17 exploded before Kelly could get out.

America badly needed a hero, and Capt Kelly was posthumously awarded the Distinguished Service Cross (DSC) and later recommended for the Medal of Honor for 'sinking' the battleship *Haruna*! This story was given out to boost morale at home, but Kelly's bravery in attacking a ship against such overwhelming odds and staying at the controls of his doomed B-17 while his crew escaped was unquestioned.

On 10 December Maj David R Gibbs assumed command of the 19th BG from Col Eubank, who moved to HQ, V Bomber Command, in Manila. That same day B-17C 40-2045 of the 14th BS was shot down over Luzon to become the first B-17 lost in combat in the Pacific. Two days later, Maj Gibbs took off in a B-17 for Mindanao and was never seen again. He was presumed killed in action. 'Rosie' O'Donnell took command of the group.

By now the Japanese had successfully established a bridgehead at

These waist gunners are smiling despite their cramped compartment in this early B-17. Note their hand-operated, K-5 post-mounted 0.50-cal machine guns, these being fed with bullets from metal ammunition boxes that each contained 100 rounds. The latter were replaced by belt feeds, with two ammunition boxes being fixed to the roof. Eventually, all machine guns were power-operated, armour plate was installed in the fuselage to help protect the gunners and, beginning with late B-17Gs, the waist positions were staggered to ease congestion in the compartment (*Boeing*)

Legaspi, on southern Luzon. On 14 December an attempt was made to bomb the invasion fleet there with six B-17Cs – a big formation at that stage. Flying lead was 1Lt James T Connally, who earlier that year had been an instructor on B-17Cs with No 90 Sqn in England.

Connally, who became Group Operations Officer, went from 1st Lieutenant to Lieutenant Colonel in three months, taking command of the 19th BG on 15 April 1942. Later in the war he led the B-29-equipped 504th BG and was killed bombing Japan in February 1945.

When Connally taxied out a tyre blew and he had to abort. The others carried on, and two of the five were so badly shot up they never made it back to the airfield. Only three reached the target area. Lt Jack Adams, who unloaded all of his bombs during the first pass, was attacked by six Zeros and crash-landed on the beach on the island of Masbate, just south of Luzon. The crew were fired on as they left the aircraft but escaped, and most eventually returned to Del Monte with the help of Filipino guerrillas. Meanwhile, Lt Elliott Vandevanter made three runs over Legaspi and returned safely to Del Monte – Vandevanter returned to the US early in 1943, assumed command of the B-17F-equipped 385th BG and took it to England in June of that year to join the Eighth Air Force.

The third B-17, piloted by 1Lt Hewitt T 'Shorty' Wheless, dropped all eight of its 600-lb bombs on shipping and was then confronted by 18 Zero fighters. They sprayed the B-17 with gunfire, killing belly gunner Pfc W G Killin and badly wounding three of the crew. Wheless kept the B-17 in the air with a series of violent evasive manoeuvres, but the aircraft was badly shot up and losing fuel. The pilot knew Del Monte was out of the question, so he headed for a small strip at Cagayan, 20 miles north-west of Del Monte. On the approach, he could see that the runway was covered with obstacles, but he had to

DSC-winning 1Lt Hewitt T 'Shorty' Wheless of the 19th BG tells Boeing workers in Seattle of his battle with 18 Zero fighters over Legaspi, on the Philippine island of Luzon, on 14 December 1941 (*USAF*)

land. The B-17 smashed its way along the strip until the brakes locked and it stood on its nose, before falling back on its tail. Shaken, the wounded crew scrambled out safely. The Fortress had been punctured by 1200 bullet holes, and Wheless was later awarded the DSC.

The decision was taken to move the surviving Fortresses of the 19th BG further south, out of range of Japanese aircraft. On 17 December 1941, some of the B-17s began evacuating Del Monte, flying 1500 miles south to Batchelor Field, Darwin, on the northern tip of Australia. Two days later the Japanese bombed Del Monte, but the B-17s that remained escaped being damaged. On the 22nd nine B-17s from Batchelor Field bombed the docks and Japanese shipping at Davao Bay, Mindanao, and claimed to have sunk a tanker, before they landed at Del Monte – fortunately still in American hands – to refuel. The following day four serviceable B-17s took off shortly after midnight and bombed Japanese transports at Lingayen Gulf, Luzon.

On the 24th three B-17s attacked the airfield and shipping at Davao before landing at Batchelor Field. That same day two Fortresses left Manila for Darwin with HQ FEAF personnel aboard. All AAF units on Luzon, as well as ground forces, then began leaving for the Bataan Peninsula. With the abandonment of the air echelon in the Philippines that day, Clark Field was evacuated – the ground echelon was re-designated as ground forces and trained as infantry.

The group was now dispersed on Bataan on Luzon, Del Monte on Mindanao (the following month Del Monte would serve as a staging area for B-17s operating out of the Netherlands East Indies against targets in the Philippines), Batchelor Field in Australia and the Dutch military field at Singosari aerodrome, near Malang in Java.

On 30 December, 759 officers and men of the 19th BG were sent by boat from Bataan to Mindanao, where they were made part of the Bisayan-Mindanao force. On 1 January 1942 Maj Cecil Combs, who was CO of the 93rd BS, assumed command of the air echelon, which was transferred to Singosari. From here raids were staged through Borneo or Celebes. Although the latter bases brought the B-17s nearer to their targets, only bomb loads under two tons could be carried

This B-17E of the 19th BG was set alight at Anchi airfield, in Java, during a Japanese strafing raid in early 1942 (*USAF*)

because an extra fuel tank had to be installed in one half of the bomb-bay. If the mission was extra long, another fuel tank was placed in the nose next to the bombardier!

With the 19th BG went remnants of the 7th BG, including the 9th BS, commanded by Capt Robert 'Pappy' Northcutt, at Madeoin in Java. Personnel who could be evacuated from the Philippines by air and submarine joined the force in Java. On 12 January Maj O'Donnell, in an old B-18 with auxiliary fuel tanks made from 50-gallon drums, flew to Australia with Lt Clyde Box as co-pilot and Lt Edwin S Green as navigator.

Six B-17s in two three-ship formations, led by Maj Cecil Combs flying as command pilot in the right-hand seat aboard Lt Connally's bomber, left Malang and staged through Samarinda, on Borneo, during 4/5 January for a raid on an airfield at Job. After bombing, they were to go on to Mindanao to pick up personnel. Crews had to fight their way through an equatorial storm, high winds and rain, as well as Zeros and anti-aircraft fire, and Job was socked in so the crews headed for the Philippines without dropping their 100-lb bombs.

As they flew over Davao Bay at 7500 ft, they could see an enemy tanker of around 15,000 tons with an escort of destroyers. Each Fortress carried seven 100-lb bombs and a fuel tank in the bomb-bay. Of the 21 bombs dropped by the first flight, one went into the sea on one side of the tanker and two the other side, while 18 bombs hit the vessel, which was probably carrying high test gasoline as it exploded in a huge ball of flame. Japanese submarines and smaller craft were also reported damaged. Flying blind through the storm, the crews returned to Borneo almost out of fuel, and refuelled for another raid.

Another strike was made on this target four days later by B-17s flying from Kendari, on the eastern side of Celebes, where in 1940 the Dutch had built the finest airfield in the Dutch East Indies. On the 11th the B-17s from Malang attacked landing forces on Tarakan.

During the afternoon of 14 January 1942, four B-17Es which were badly needed by the 7th BG arrived at Kendari after flying a tortuous route from the USA. The aircraft, which had all left MacDill, in Florida, on Christmas Day 1941, were 41-2406 flown by Maj Kenneth B Hobson and 41-2419 flown by 1Lt J W Hughes, both from the 22nd BS, and 41-2461 piloted by Maj Conrad E Necrason and 41-2459 piloted by 1Lt J L 'Duke' Du Frane, both from the 9th BS.

On 16 January two of these B-17Es raided Japanese shipping in Manado Bay – the most northerly point of the Celebes Islands – while three LB-30 Liberators hit Langoan aerodrome, 20 miles south. All of them staged through Kendari II. The mission was flown at the behest of Field Marshal Sir Archibald Wavell, the supreme commander of Allied forces in the area, who badly needed a morale boost for his beleaguered British troops in Singapore.

At 0440 hrs the two B-17Es – Maj Necrason's 41-2461 *El Toro*, with 1Lt Bernice 'Bernie' Barr as co-pilot, and 41-2459, flown by 1Lt Du Frane, with 1Lt R V W Negley as co-pilot – departed Malang, along with the three LB-30s. They landed at Kendari II at 0845 hrs and the aircraft were serviced with gasoline and bombs. The LB-30s were each loaded with 12 bombs of 220 lbs and each B-17E with ten.

At 1915 hrs the five aircraft took off from Kendari II and headed for their targets. The LB-30s bombed the aerodrome at Langoan from 19,500 ft at 2236 hrs. Hits were made on the runway and dispersal areas. Between 2309 and 2315 hrs, the three Liberators were attacked by five Zero fighters. One of the bombers, piloted by Lt Basye, was forced down at Makassar, on the Celebes. Two crewmen were injured and the bomber was damaged beyond repair.

Meanwhile, the two B-17Es reached Manado Bay at 2230 hrs. Two large and two small transports were spotted, while two others were tied up at Manado dock. Necrason and Du Frane began their runs on the four transports, but the sun on the first run hampered visibility and no bombs were dropped. On the second run hits were claimed on a large vessel, which sank, although six 220-lb bombs in one B-17E failed to drop. Two of these were dropped on the runway at Langoan but the remaining four remained in the bomb-bay.

Five minutes after the attack, enemy fighters were seen climbing. For 45 minutes from 2240 hrs, 15 Zeros attacked from the rear of the B-17Es, diving under the bombers and pulling up to fire. However, the enemy pilots were in for a shock, as 1Lt Barr recalls;

'These were the first two B-17s that had ever gone into combat with tail guns in them. None of the older B-17s had these guns, and the Japanese Zero pilots had learned to come up and slip in behind a B-17, fire, and with their faster speed overtake, all without even being shot at. However, this time we were armed in this quarter, and of course the Zero pilots did not know it. As they came in to attack our tail gunner, Pte A B Hegdahl, shot two of them down. Their approach – from below the aeroplane, from the tail, from the side and from the top – all took place at about 26,000 ft.

'This fight resulted in our gunners shooting down five Zeros. We got quite a few holes in our aeroplanes, but not enough to knock us out of the air. Pte Hegdahl was seriously wounded in the knee by an explosive bullet. M/Sgt Silva, our flight engineer, left his gun position and removed him from the tail position and gave him first aid and a shot of pain reliever.'

In all, six Zeros were claimed shot down during the air battle, five falling to Necrason's crew. Du Frane's Fortress had two engines put out of action, but both he and Necrason managed to keep the

A rather ineffective 0.30-cal machine gun could be mounted in sockets in the nose of the E- and F-model Fortresses for operation by the bombardier and navigator. Three sockets, including one non-standard fitting in the roof, can be seen in this B-17E pictured in the US. Note also the early ring-and-bead sight atop the Browning and the empty side magazine (*USAF*)

machines airborne and they put down safely at Kendari II at 0100 hrs on 17 January to refuel. Fuel was pumped into the two B-17s by hand from 55-gallon drums. At 0215 hrs *El Toro* was half refuelled when the siren sounded. Lt Bernie Barr was helping a Dutch doctor apply compresses and splints to Hegdahl's leg when Zeros suddenly attacked the grass field and badly damaged Du Frane's B-17. Barr recalls;

'This was one heck of a spot to be in! Necrason ordered the crew to button up the aeroplane for immediate take-off. We started without warming up or checking the engines – no time for warm-up. Necrason began the take-off roll across the grass field. As I raised the landing gear, after having set the superchargers during the take-off roll, five Zero fighters attacked us from the rear. As we got about five feet off the ground, bullets came roaring through the aeroplane all the way from the tail, and up, through the cockpit over the pilot's and my head. The cockpit was filled with crashing, exploding bullets, which were creasing the pilot's and my hair. Over half of the instruments were knocked out and they removed over half of the windshield in front of Necrason, but the good old aeroplane stayed in the air.

'After several more damaging attacks from the Zeros we were able to escape into a nearby thunderstorm about ten miles from Kendari, dodging and using evasive action low over the ground until we got into the clouds. The fighters lost us. It then took us six hours to fly back to Malang, where Hegdahl was immediately taken to the city hospital for treatment. I last saw him on 22 January. He was in traction in his hospital bed and could not be moved. Later, when we evacuated Java on a few hours' notice, we could only load combat crews into the remaining B-17s and fly to Australia. Hegdahl was one of those left behind.'

Meanwhile, the Zeros returned to the other B-17, which had been unable to get off the ground, and set it alight with their gunfire. 'Duke' Du Frane's aircraft was later blown up during the US retreat.

Armourers hastily load 100- and 500-lb bombs into the bomb-bay of a B-17D either in the Philippines or the Dutch East Indies during the first weeks of the war in the Pacific (*USAF*)

B-17D 40-3097 *"THE SWOOSE"* was named after a popular song of the time which referred to Alexander, who was half swan and half goose. Assigned to the 19th BG at Hickam Field, Hawaii, on 14 May 1941, the aircraft fought in Java from 30 December 1941, before being used as a personal 'hack' for Lt Gen George M Brett, CO Allied Air Forces in Australia. It returned to the USA with Brett in August 1942 and was placed in storage at Kingman, Arizona in 1945. Astoundingly, the veteran bomber escaped being scrapped post-war and is currently stored in the National Air and Space Museum's Paul Garber facility in Maryland. 40-3097 is the oldest known surviving B-17, and the only D-model in existence (*USAF*)

At 1315 hrs a LB-30 piloted by Lt Wade set out to pick up Du Frane's crew. 'Duke' and his men were duly collected and returned at 0730 hrs on 19 January. Two of the crew had suffered minor arm injuries and were treated in hospital. Du Frane was subsequently awarded the DSC. His citation stated that his crew had sunk a transport and shot down seven Zeros – in fact, they had claimed only one.

On 18 January B-17E 41-2468, flown by 1Lt Robert 'Pappy' E Northcutt and 2Lt Melvin G Pfund, arrived at Kendari – this Fortress enjoyed only the briefest of careers, being lost just seven days later when Northcutt was forced to crash-land in the Madera Islands. The 19th saw six Fortresses, led by Lt Connally, fly through a driving rainstorm and fog in order to mount a surprise raid on Japanese vessels off the island of Jolo. They later landed in the dark, and the rain, at Del Monte, where the crews picked up 20 combat pilots who had struggled through from Clark Field. Within a day these men were flying B-17s from Java. On 24 January a Japanese invasion force landed at Kendari. Ambon, an island to the east, was invaded on 30 January and the Japanese quickly overran the defenders.

From 22 January to 3 February, the B-17s launched at least 15 missions out of Malang against enemy shipping moving through the Makassar Strait. Four were aborted because of bad weather, six proved negative and the remaining five resulted in heavy losses. However, four ships were believed sunk. From now on bad weather and effective Japanese fighter interceptions prevented the Fortresses from delivering any worthwhile strikes on the all-conquering Japanese forces.

By the end of January the Japanese had landed at Lae, in New Guinea, in several places on Borneo and in Rabaul, New Britain, where air bases for extending Japanese air operations were constructed. On 3 February Port Moresby, capital of New Guinea, was bombed, but despite fears of a Japanese invasion, it managed to hold out.

However, the situation in Java was perilous. To save their B-17s, pilots and crews took extraordinary risks. In one raid the Japanese caught a Fortress on the ground and it seemed doomed. However, Capt Dean Hovet, a communications expert who had been brought from Bataan to Java in a submarine, dashed to the B-17 and took off with only two engines running. For 20 minutes he hedge-hopped trees and brush, twisting and banking like a fighter, and managed to evade the fighters until their ammunition was spent. Lt Bernie Barr recalls;

'Every day we had sirens going and people were low on morale, on equipment and the like. Between the missions, if there were no Japanese around, the Dutch, who were in control of Java at the time, had a pretty good system going. They had good ice cream, peach Melbas and movies from the US, so when we weren't busy going on a mission or a training exercise, we could escape for a few hours and go into town. Jakarta was the first one that I became acquainted with. We enjoyed life. But then you had to get ready to fly a mission. You went out and got your crew and your course and altitude briefings and the target. It became a little dangerous when Zeros came humming around you like bees. We lost a lot of aircraft during these missions.

'My God, we didn't know whether we were going to get out of Java or not. The morning after the Japanese invasion I was in the operations room, located in the hangar where the aeroplanes were maintained ready to be dispatched on the day's mission, when the siren went off. I ran into the middle of the hangar and started for a trench to jump into. In the meantime, Zeros were firing into the hangar. All I could do was fall flat on my face on to the concrete floor and hope to God that the bullets would miss me, which they did.

'So after three or four passes they left and I was able to get out of the hangar. Then later in the day they came over with bombers and dropped bombs on the airfield. I jumped into my aeroplane and flew to the south of Java to escape the attack. After it was all clear we came back and landed, loading up the aeroplanes with bombs.

An excellent view of the 0.50-cal machine gun which was installed in the radio room of B-17E/Fs for rear defence (*USAF*)

'At 0300 hrs we took off again to bomb Japanese ships that were unloading troops on the north shore of Java. We visually bombed the vessels by moonlight. The crew told me that we hit two of them. There were only a few Dutch troops available to meet the Japanese as they invaded, so the enemy had a clear run to all of the major cities in Java.'

There were not enough aircraft to stem the Japanese tide, which had now consumed the entire Netherlands East Indies, as well as the Philippines. Gen Douglas MacArthur, commander-in-chief in the Philippines, sought shelter in the Malinta Tunnel on Corregidor. On 22 February he received a signal from President Roosevelt ordering him to leave his position and proceed to Australia to assume command of all US troops.

A 7th BG B-17E has its starboard inner Wright R-1820-97 Cyclone radial engine serviced between missions on a Javanese airfield (*USAF*)

On the 27th the evacuation of Java to Australia began. Most of the B-17Es of the 7th and 19th BGs that were flyable were made ready to depart. In the 7th BG only four combat serviceable B-17s and four combat crews – Capt Clayton Beran and 41-2452 (this aircraft was later ditched off New Guinea on 10 August 1942), Lt Barr and 41-2461, Lt Richard Beck and 41-2416 *San Antonio Rose II* and Capt Felix Hardison and 41-2464 – remained at Madioén. These crews did all their own maintenance work on the B-17s, serviced them with fuel and loaded them with bombs. They

Lt John H Pius's crew pose in front of veteran B-17E 41-2416 *SAN ANTONIO ROSE* of the 98th BS/11th BG at Koomac, on New Caledonia, in August 1942. Later transferred to the 88th RS/7th BG, *San Antonio Rose* had earlier suffered structural damage during a rough landing at Townsville on 22 February 1942 (*Mrs Pius via Bill Cleveland*)

also took the Fortresses aloft during air raids to prevent them being destroyed on the ground by air attacks. All this was done with very little rest and practically no food.

During the night of 28 February-1 March, the four crews carried out bombing attacks on the Japanese invasion fleet landing troops on Java's north coast. Capt Beran's crew loaded their bombs after dark, and just after midnight took off to attack the enemy convoy off the coast at Rembang. They made two runs and claimed hits on a large transport, which was believed sunk. Returning to Madioén, the crew carried out maintenance or flew air raid alarm missions all day. After dark on 1 March they prepared the B-17 to leave Java, and took off at midnight fully loaded with evacuees. They landed at Broome, Australia, and the next morning serviced the bomber and flew on to Perth.

Meanwhile, on 28 February Lt Barr's crew flew air alert missions for most of the day and landed at Madioén at sunset. They immediately carried out the necessary maintenance work on the B-17 and loaded bombs for an attack on the invasion convoy. Taking off just after midnight, they flew over the vessels off Rembang and released bombs on two out of three runs. Two ships were left burning and listing badly. Returning to Madioén at sunrise, the crew went without breakfast as none was available. Maintenance work was performed, plus the air alarm flights to avoid Japanese raids. Loaded for evacuation, 41-2461 (which was destroyed in an attack on Port Moresby on 25 April 1942) took off after midnight, landing at Broome early on the morning of 1 March. This time the crew had breakfast, and flew on to Perth.

On 28 February Lt Beck's crew worked on maintenance whenever they were not flying air alarm alerts. They loaded their bombs and after midnight took off to attack the Japanese fleet. During runs over the convoy they were twice driven off by anti-aircraft fire, but they pressed on and dropped bombs on the third run. The results could not be seen due to cloud cover and intense anti-aircraft fire from the fleet. After landing back at Madioén at 0400 hrs the maintenance work began. Six times that day it was interrupted by enemy air attack, and each time the B-17 took off to avoid destruction.

At 1800 hrs Beck's crew took off for Jakarta, where they loaded 25 passengers and headed off at midnight for Broome. On 3 March, with the same plane-load of passengers, they left Broome only 18 minutes before the Japanese carried out a devastating air attack on the town and aerodrome. 41-2417 *San Antonio Rose II*, with Lt Thompson's crew on board, crashed in Queensland on 6 July 1942 and was written off.

Capt Felix Hardison wrote of the events;

The tail-gun station on a B-17E photographed on the Boeing production line on 1 October 1941. This view shows the early style ring-and-bead sight mounted outside the window, which was replaced on Fortresses two years later by an internal reflector sight. In the Pacific, Japanese fighter pilots who had grown accustomed to attacking early Fortresses from the rear received an unpleasant shock when they came up against the rear gun installation fitted to B-17Es for the first time. Prior to the arrival of tail guns, Fortress pilots had learned to compensate for this weakness by jinking their aircraft back and forth when being attacked from the rear, alternatively giving the left and right waist gunners a shot at the approaching fighters (*Boeing*)

'Subject to air raid alarms all day (28 February), and the crew did maintenance work on the ship until midnight, then serviced with fuel and eight 300-kg (661-lb) bombs for bombing the Japanese landing target areas off Rembang, Java. Took off at 0245 hrs on 1 March – arriving over the target area, found it obscured by large thunderheads. We let down through the clouds to an altitude of 3000 ft over the target area and opened our bomb-bay doors.

'The moon had set earlier, and due to pitch dark under the clouds we were unable to pick up a target, except for occasional flashes of pocket torches. We flew back and forth over the target two times inviting searchlights, but finally decided to wait for dawn rather than waste our bombs. Circled a point of land near Rembang to keep from getting lost until first light. Took us longer to arrive back over the target than we anticipated – the sun was rising while on our run at 3800 ft indicated. Found the enemy lying about one half-mile off the coast – transports in two parallel rows, with warships forming a protective screen.

'Twice co-pilot Lt Ellsworth McRoberts counted 57 transports and warships. Troops and equipment were going ashore in self-propelled barges, which the gunners engaged throughout the run and withdrawal, inflicting some casualties and damage. M/Sgt David Semple, the bombardier, picked one of the largest transports to bomb, getting several near misses and one direct hit. Some difficulty was experienced in following the Positional Direction Indicator because of near misses from anti-aircraft fire – several tracers penetrated the ship but no material damage was sustained by either men or aeroplane. The bombed vessel was last seen listing badly to starboard, believed to be sinking.

'Returned to Madioén, where the crew underwent six air alarms during the day. Took off early on 2 March for Broome with 25 men aboard. Departed Broome after dark, flying direct to Melbourne. It is with pride that I recall the exemplary action. The esprit de corps and the willingness for duty shown by the officers and men at Madioén during the period mentioned was typical of the real fighting USAAC.'

41-2464 later served in the 43rd BG before being named *Queenie* and used as a Fifth Air Force Service Command 'hack'. It was lost on 8 July 1944 with 19 personnel aboard.

Despite the bravery and dedication of the US airmen as they tried to turn back the Japanese invasion of Java, the AAF did not slow the enemy advance. In the end the Japanese captured many of the Indonesian Islands and the Philippines. However, the effectiveness that the B-17s showed in bombing invasion fleets proved that an attempted invasion of Australia would have been hazardous or even disastrous.

When asked about the Army Air Forces' contribution to the war against the Japanese in the Pacific, 1Lt Bernie Barr replied;

'I think we did a lot to hold back the invasion of Australia, even though the Japanese did continue their invasion of the Solomon Islands down to Guadalcanal. It was a hell of a battle for the Marines and the Army to kick them out. We wanted to defend all of those islands, Java, the Celebes and the Philippines, but we were not prepared to do so. But we were risking our lives every day flying out on these missions against their fighters and their ground anti-aircraft guns.'

The courage and bravery shown by the men of the 7th and 19th BGs during their battles in the South Pacific was remarkable. Fighting in a war when well equipped and prepared is testing enough on the psyche and body, but doing so while ill prepared and under equipped is quite another matter that requires great stamina and strength of character. These men did the best possible job under conditions that neither nurtured high morale nor made success seem attainable.

The same fate that befell the 7th BG in the Philippines befell the 19th BG. On 5 February 1942 the Japanese began moving their aircraft into Ambon to strengthen their air superiority in the area. Nine B-17s from the hard-pressed 19th were despatched to Kendari, the formation climbing slowly through heavy clouds. At 15,000 ft they broke out on top – and ran straight into a horde of Zeros. 'Duke' Du Frane's B-17 went down in flames, while the bomber piloted by Lt W T Pritchard swung around in a wild turn and almost crashed into a Zero. Tracers ripped into the B-17, which plunged into the clouds on fire.

Lt Lindsey made a skidding turn and kicked his B-17 into the cloud top as tracers ripped into the Fortress. Losing speed, the half-crippled B-17 fell off into a tailspin, and at 9000 ft it was still spinning. The co-pilot and navigator scrambled aft and baled out through the open bomb-bay, and the rest of the crew were about to follow when Lindsey miraculously recovered from the spin and pulled the nose up. Circling down carefully, he looked out across the barren Java Sea. There was no sign of the two crew in the water. With his compass and other instruments shot away, Lindsey battled with the badly damaged Fortress through a tropical storm and landed back at base.

When Palembang fell on 16 February 1942, no replacements could get through to the beleaguered 19th BG.

On paper the Army Air Forces had 12,000 aircraft of all types, of which 913 combat models, including 61 B-17s and B-24s, were spread very thinly overseas in Alaska, Iceland, Greenland, Panama, Newfoundland, Hawaii and the Philippines. Thirteen groups were equipped with the B-17, but most were well below the group strength of 32 aircraft. Some 150 B-17s of all models, including 12 YB-17s, were scattered along the Pacific seaboard, Alaska and Newfoundland.

The few ground mechanics in Java did heroic work, driving themselves to exhaustion. B-17s returning from bombing raids had to make forced landings miles away from their airfields. If wrecked beyond repair, crews tore out badly needed parts and carried them to their base, otherwise salvage crews went out by truck and brought back the priceless parts. 'Wrecker' pilots such as Lt Clare McPherson risked their lives to fly disabled B-17s out of clearings where their original pilots had barely been able to land. There were other remarkable feats too, including Lt Philip Mathewson's lone attacks on Japanese targets.

The Japanese were only 35 miles away, and with anti-aircraft fire along the coast, crews had to climb to 35,000 ft, if they could get that high, to avoid enemy fire. Col Eubank realised that resistance was futile, and on 24 February, with the enemy only 20 minutes away, ordered the few remaining B-17s in Java to head for Australia. Not all of them made it – on 25 February B-17E 41-2406, flown by Maj Kenneth B Hobson, crash-landed on Madera Island.

ON WINGS WE CONQUER

In Australia, the remnants of the 88th BS/7th BG, some crews from the 11th BG and one pick-up crew were used to bring the 19th BG back up to strength – the 7th BG was subsequently reorganised in India and the group converted to B-24s. The 19th BG was further strengthened with the arrival of six crews from the 22nd BS/7th BG, commanded by Maj Richard N Carmichael, which were sent from Hawaii to Australia. Lt Harry Spieth's crew was one of the half dozen which would now become the famous 435th 'Kangaroo' BS of the 19th BG. His co pilot, Lt John Fields, recalls;

'The first leg was to tropical Christmas Island. The strips that we landed on were made of crushed coral, rolled and packed by a group of engineers from Hawaii. It was here that I saw my first green coconut and learned that it would do very nicely in place of a laxative! We left Christmas Island on 12 January 1942 and made an eight-hour flight to Canton Island, a small coral atoll in the Pacific which had only one tree and one landing strip. This landing strip had numerous gooney birds on it. The personnel on Canton had everything underground.

'We went on to Fiji and spent a weekend waiting for the Free French to chase the Vichy French in New Caledonia up into the hills before we could land at Plindegaig. We got in and refuelled, but we had to get off again because we were not particularly safe there. We flew on into Townsville, Australia, and arrived there around 2000 hrs. The Australians thought that their great saviours had arrived when we tooled in there in the first B-17Es that they had ever seen! Truthfully, they were afraid that the Japs were going to move in and take Australia, and this was a possibility for several months.'

The B-17Es initially used Garbutt Field near Townsville, before being dispersed to Charters Towers, some 50 miles away, and to Cloncurry 300 miles from Townsville.

On 22 February 1942, nine B-17Es of the 435th BS taxied out for an attack on Rabaul Harbour in New Britain. Rabaul was to be the jumping-off point for the Japanese invasion of New Guinea, and

Harry Spieth's 7th BG crew. Standing, from left to right, are Golden (assistant radio operator and waist gunner), Hall (radio operator), Panosian (assistant flight engineer and waist gunner), Ottaviano (tail gunner) and Clark (ball turret gunner). Kneeling, from left to right, are Stashuk (crew chief and top turret gunner), Hulet Hornbeck (navigator), Lt Harry Spieth (pilot) and Lt John Wallace Fields (co-pilot) (*via Ken Fields*)

A lone B-17E of the Pacific Air Forces is seen parked between missions at its dispersal at Mareeba, in northern Queensland, in 1942 (*USAF*)

A rare Douglas DC-5 transport departs Port Moresby on 19 August 1942 while B-17Es 41-9208 (foreground) and 41-2659 *Frank Buck* (*Bring 'Em Back Alive*) of the 28th BS/19th BG are prepared for their next mission. 41-9208 crashed on take off from Port Moresby on 19 September 1942 and was wrecked. The DC-5 was one three ex-Dutch aircraft used by the Allied Directorate of Air Transport, designated the C-110 by the USAAF (*USAF*)

On 22 February 1942 nine B-17Es of the 435th BS/19th BG taxied out at Townsville for an attack on Rabaul Harbour. Two Fortresses, piloted by Deacon Rawls and Frank Bostrom, hit each other in the pre-dawn darkness (*www.aerothentic.com*)

further, Australia and New Zealand. Two Fortresses, piloted by Deacon Rawls and Frank Bostrom, taxied into each other in the pre-dawn darkness, and a third suffered mechanical problems, leaving six airworthy B-17s. These newly minted B-17Es, led by Maj Carmichael, left Townsville on 23 February for an early morning rendezvous over Magnetic Island, and then across the Coral Sea, New Guinea and the Solomon Sea to Rabaul. A return refuelling stop at Port Moresby capped their hastily planned mission of some 13 hours' duration.

Ninety miles out, the formation was broken up by severe weather – Harry Spieth's crew could not get through it and had to return after about nine hours. Capt Bill Lewis, who was leading the second echelon, and Lt Fred Eaton in 41-2446 were able to locate their target first. Eaton lingered over Rabaul

Harbour for half an hour looking for an opening in the clouds through which to commence his bomb run. He was finally able to pick out several large Japanese troop transports and make his attack, but was unable to get his bombs away so a second run was made. This time the bombs salvoed, although he was unable to observe the result. During the bomb run, a Japanese anti-aircraft shell came straight up through the right wing near the outboard

engine, not exploding until it was already through the wing. The concussion violently knocked the wing down but did no other damage.

By now as many as 12 Zeros had reached the B-17's altitude, and they began a series of gunnery passes. At 0745 hrs the first enemy fighter was shot down by tail gunner Sgt J V Hall. Waist gunner Sgt Russell Crawford then destroyed a second Zero and Sgt Hall hit a third fighter, which was seen to lose altitude but could not be confirmed as having crashed. The air battle continued for more than 40 minutes as Eaton jockeyed the B-17 from cloud to cloud, trying to evade enemy fire. The vertical stabiliser and radio operator's compartment were hit by both 20 mm cannon and machine gun rounds.

The long wait over the target, the two bomb runs, all the evasive manoeuvres and the battle damage led to Eaton running short of fuel just over the eastern coast of New Guinea. He realised he would never make Port Moresby, situated on the far coast and across the treacherous Owen Stanley Range, so decided to set the B-17 down in what appeared to be a level field some eight miles inland. He feathered the two inboard engines and all the crew except Eaton himself, co-pilot Henry Harlow and engineer Sgt Clarence Lemieux took up crash positions in the radio operator's compartment. The B-17 came in neatly, but as it levelled out Eaton was shocked to realise he was landing in a kunai grass-filled reservoir of water five to six feet deep – the Agiambo Swamp. The B-17 did a slow 90-degree turn to the right as it settled into its last resting-place, where it still remains at the time of writing.

The only injury was to navigator George Munro (a pilot pressed into service as a result of a shortage of qualified navigators), who cut his head. The crew carefully removed the Norden bombsight, placed it on the right wing and destroyed it with 0.45-cal pistol fire before tossing it into the swamp. They then set off on a cruel trek out of the swamp through the water and razor-sharp kunai grass. The men encountered huge leeches and spiders, and heard crocodiles thrashing about. Six weeks later, with the aid of Australian coast watchers, they returned to Port Moresby and went back to fighting the Japanese.

A mission on 1 March 1942 was called off, and crews were sent to Cloncurry for dispersal. At 1000 hrs on the 3rd, the Japanese attacked the airfield and harbour at Broome, in Western Australia, shortly after eight B-17s had flown in, wreaking havoc. Two Fortresses were

B-17E *WELL GODDAM* flew a number of missions from New Guinea and Australia. Here, it is seen having a multiple engine change out in the open at Mareeba (*www.aerothentic.com*)

The tail section of Lt Fred Eaton's bullet-riddled B-17E 41-2446, which crashed into a grass-covered swamp in New Guinea after a six-ship attack on Rabaul on 23 February 1942. The Fortress, from the 435th BS/7th BG, based at Townsville, in Queensland, ran out of fuel before reaching Port Moresby, forcing its pilot to ditch into Agiambo Swamp. The crew, who survived the crash-landing uninjured, were picked up by an Australian coast watcher and returned to Port Moresby on 1 April. Having come down eight miles inland from the coast of New Guinea, 41-2446 was located almost four decades later by a passing Royal Australian Air Force helicopter crew. In 1980 the site was visited by surviving members of Eaton's crew, and officials of the Papuan Historical Museum. The Historical Society of Travis AFB, in California, have expressed an interest in returning the 'Swamp Ghost', as it is now called, to the US, as it is the only B-17 left in the world in its original combat configuration (*Kenneth W Fields*)

B-17E 41-2435 of the 40th BS/19th BG flies over the Owen Stanley Range in early 1942. Note the bomber's impractical remote-controlled Bendix underfuselage turret, which was operated by a gunner lying prone to its rear, who sighted its guns through a system of mirrors contained in a small transparent blister. Two low-slit windows on both sides of the fuselage were located for the gunner to identify his target. 41-2435 was shot down off Buna on 12 August 1942 (*Ken Fields*)

Bombs dropped by a formation of B-17s explode on, and around, the airfield at Lae, in New Guinea, in early 1942 (*USAF*)

destroyed, along with 16 other aircraft, and 45 Dutch civilians and 20 US airmen were killed. Meanwhile, at Cloncurry, six crewmen had immediately gone down with dengue fever, John Fields being one of them. After recovering, he flew his second mission;

'We left Cloncurry on 11 March for Townsville, and on the 12th we left for Port Moresby for a patrol mission on the 13th to Lae, where we dropped our bombs. When we flew out of Port Moresby, which was about a two-and-a-half-hour flight from Townsville, we lived in grass huts that the natives had built, and flew off a runway that was metal stripping placed on swampy ground. We had a grass hut mess hall and had to do our own aircraft servicing. We serviced the aircraft from barrels of gas that were dumped off the ships and floated onto the shore by the natives, and we had a little gasoline pump that we used to pump the gas out of the barrel into the aeroplane. We could have used the fuel transfer pump from the aircraft itself, but we didn't like to do this because we knew we might need that fuel transfer pump in flight and we didn't want to wear it out because some of these flights involved filling up with 2400 gallons of gas.

'We would fly a mission, or two or three, out of Port Moresby, or occasionally out of Townsville, and then we would come back and go to the bottom of the list, and our turn would come up again later. In truth, it didn't always work out this way, although in principle it was supposed to. We found out early on that if you were married and had a family, then you would often be excused from flying the tougher missions. These became the reserve of the younger, unmarried men on the list. You simply moved up the list faster if you were single than you did if you were married.

'On 18 March we flew a mission to Rabaul Harbour – there were only three aircraft and we flew at an altitude of 31,000 ft. We didn't encounter any fighter aircraft. We didn't learn until the next day how much damage we had inflicted, but we had hit a large Japanese cruiser from 600 ft, blowing the stern off it. Two days later I flew with Morrie Horgan to Lae, a stronghold on the north-eastern side of the mountains of New Guinea. We destroyed 17 aircraft on the ground.

'On 24 March I went to the theatre at Charters Towers, but we were called out to go back to Townsville, and the rumour was that we were going to the Philippines. We got to Townsville on 25 March, and sure enough we had orders to go to the Philippines on an evacuation flight.

'We left Darwin's Batchelor Field on the 26th for Del Monte, on Mindanao. At that time Mindanao was in Japanese hands, with the exception of the airstrip adjacent to the Del Monte pineapple plantation. Our job was to bring out Manuel Quezon, President of the Philippines, Gens Valdez and Romulo and some of MacArthur's staff (MacArthur and his family, Adm Rockwell, Gens George and Sutherland and 14 staff members, had been evacuated from Corregidor by four PT boats to Mindanao, where, on 12 March, they were flown from Del Monte to Darwin by Frank P Bostrom – author). MacArthur sent word ahead that he wanted an airliner to meet him at Darwin to take him

to Alice Springs, and from Alice Springs he got on a train and went on to Melbourne. It took him four days to get there, when we could have had him there in eight hours!

'The flight was long and tiring. We were scheduled to land during the hours of darkness at Del Monte, which we did. They had no lights on the runway, with the exception of smudge pots which they lit for us to line up on on the grass field in the direction that we were supposed to land. These were old highway markers that looked like a bomb, the black smudge pots burning diesel fuel – they were extinguished just as soon as we had landed. We serviced our aeroplane and ate wonderful pineapple and drank plenty of beer. Then they began to assign us the various people who were scheduled to go back with us.

'Those with priority were Gen MacArthur's staff, of which there were not very many, President Quezon's family and nurse, his chief of staff Gen Romulo and one of his advisers, Gen Valdez. A small staff

Japanese shipping and oil installations at Simpson Harbour come under attack from B-17s in mid-1942. Along with Lae, the tactically important Simpson Harbour was routinely targeted by American heavy bombers in-theatre (*USAF*)

B-17E 41-2633 *Sally* and three other Fortresses from the 19th BG head for the Japanese airfield at Lae on 26-27 June 1942. 41-2633 later served as Gen Kenney's VIP transport (see page 70) (*USAF*)

went with the Philippine generals, and the next priority was the aircraft mechanics. So we filled our planes with people according to these priorities, and for whom we had parachutes.

'Others were crying, wanting to be smuggled aboard, but we had to tell them we couldn't take them as we didn't have parachutes for them. Then they would say, "Well, don't worry about a parachute. I don't need one. I won't use one" – anything to get on the aeroplane and get off the island.

'We flew for 32 hours in the next 36, firstly flying back to Darwin, where we gassed up and went on to Alice Springs. On the way there Dubose ran out of gas – he had President Quezon's nurse aboard. Luckily, he was able to land in the middle of the country. We searched for him for five hours before the other aeroplane in the flight located him. They landed and pumped fuel over into his B-17.

'The Philippine rescue flight ended in Melbourne. We had had engine trouble and had blown two cylinders, so they told us to stay there and change all four engines before we went back to Townsville. We spent 26 days getting the engines changed out. Del Monte held out for another ten days after we left.'

Within a month of the surrender of US forces in the Philippines, a force of ten B-25s and three B-17s attacked Del Monte from Darwin. One of the Fortresses also attacked Japanese-occupied Manila at night but its bombs exploded harmlessly in the bay.

By mid-April 1942 the Japanese were well on their way to total domination in the New Guinea-New Britain-Solomon Islands area of the South Pacific. By mid-May they had overrun the Bataan Peninsula, the island fortress of Corregidor and the last two outposts on Luzon, as well as having driven the Allies out of Burma.

Japanese expansion was finally checked when an invasion fleet heading for Port Moresby was defeated in the Battle of the Coral Sea – the first battle in history in which opposing naval forces had not exchanged gunfire, instead trading blows with carrier-launched aircraft.

Taken on the same mission as the photograph at the bottom of the opposite page, this shot shows B-17E 41-2633 *Sally* and three other Fortresses heading for Lae on 26-27 June 1942. The B-17E nearest *Sally*'s tail is 41-2461, piloted by Lt Bernice 'Bernie' Barr, who had taken over the bomber's crew from Maj Conrad E Necrason when the latter had been ordered to India for further duty (*USAF*)

Lt Gen George C Kenney (left) presents Lt John W Fields with the Distinguished Flying Cross at Townsville following his Philippines rescue mission of 26 March 1942 (*via Ken Fields*)

The 19th BG raided Japanese targets during the invasion of New Guinea. John Fields recalls;

'We could tell from the number of surface vessels that were coming into the area and congregating there that a big naval battle was shaping up. We flew missions out of Townsville on 6, 7, 8 and 11 May. On the 6th we found the Japanese fleet – we sighted an aircraft carrier and made a run on it. We were in the same flight as "Hotfoot" Harlow, who bombed a heavy cruiser. Wilbur Beezley was flying with us, too. We had heavy anti-aircraft fire, but few fighters, as they were all carrier-based – their fighters were too busy with the US Navy and the low-level stuff.

'On one of our Coral Sea missions there was a bit of confusion. The Navy had told us that everything north of a certain parallel would be friendly. We were north of this line, and there was a squadron of B-26s on the mission with us too. We came in at about 18,000 ft and could see some aeroplanes flying below and diving at low level. We thought these were the B-26s, so we lined up on the vessel that they were bombing and dropped our bombs on it. It turned out to be the Australian flagship HMS *Australia*, and the aeroplanes we saw diving were Jap bombers! Luckily we didn't hit it and they didn't hit us.'

The 93rd BS/19th BG was sent to Longreach, Queensland, in May 1942. The CO, Maj Hardison, had flown 41-2489 *SUZY-Q* (a new B-17E named after his wife) into Java during February. Once in Australia, two of Hardison's original gunners went sick and the replacements were two old-timers, John Geckeler and Bill Bostwick. Hardison's bombardier had been killed in an air raid just prior to the evacuation to Australia and Durwood Fesmire became his bombardier. He later recalled;

'My trial period took in four missions in four days. On the first we bombed a ship off Timor. Our navigator passed out through lack of oxygen, collapsing on his table during the bomb run, so after we'd dropped I had to go back and take care of him. He made it all right. We had a general with us that day. He was looking out of the bomb-bay and he said we hit the ship.

'Next day we went back to the same (*text continues on page 49*)

B-17E 41-2632 *CROCK O' CRAP* served with the 93rd BS/19th BG. Delivered to Lowry Modification Center in Colorado on 5 March, and then based at Boise, Idaho, from 7 April 1942, it was assigned to the Seventh Air Force in Hawaii on 28 May 1942. Having survived a long tour of duty in the South-West Pacific (including appearing in the classic John Ford war film on Midway), *CROC O' CRAP* returned to the US on 21 December 1943. It eventually wound up in the Reclamation Finance Center (RFC) storage facility in Albuquerque on 9 August 1945, where the bomber was duly scrapped (*www.aerothentic.com*)

Promoted to aircraft commander during the course of his combat tour, Lt John W Fields led these men for much of his time in the South-West Pacific. They are, standing, from left to right, Nibley (a former crewmember), Skinner (ball turret gunner), Ravenscroft (waist gunner), Rohr (radio operator), Klimpel (crew chief) and Stark (waist gunner). Kneeling, from left to right, Mickakaeles (tail gunner), Morton (bombardier), Hulet Hornbeck (navigator), Stanley Casey (co-pilot) and Lt Fields (pilot) (*via Ken Fields*)

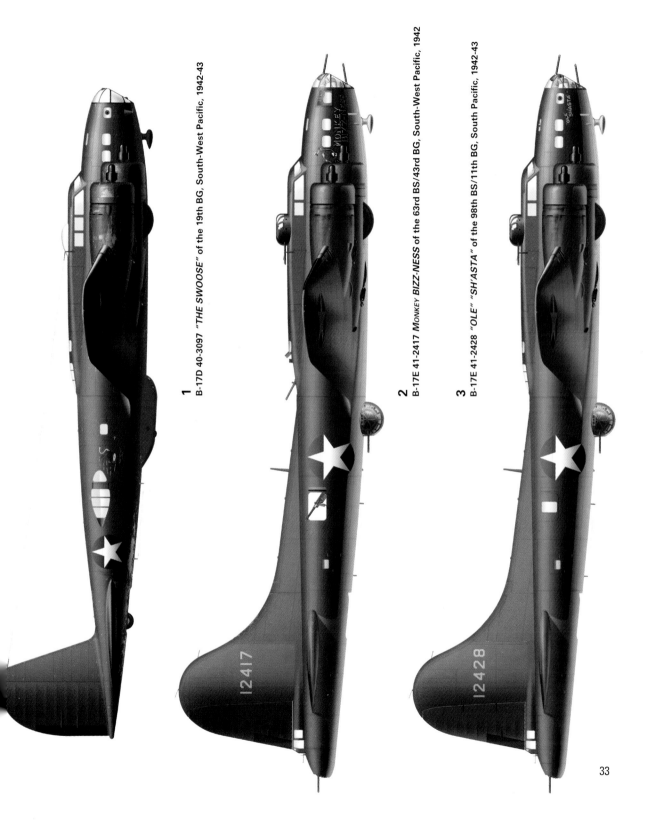

1
B-17D 40-3097 *"THE SWOOSE"* of the 19th BG, South-West Pacific, 1942-43

2
B-17E 41-2417 Monkey *BIZZ-NESS* of the 63rd BS/43rd BG, South-West Pacific, 1942

3
B-17E 41-2428 *"OLE" "SH'ASTA"* of the 98th BS/11th BG, South Pacific, 1942-43

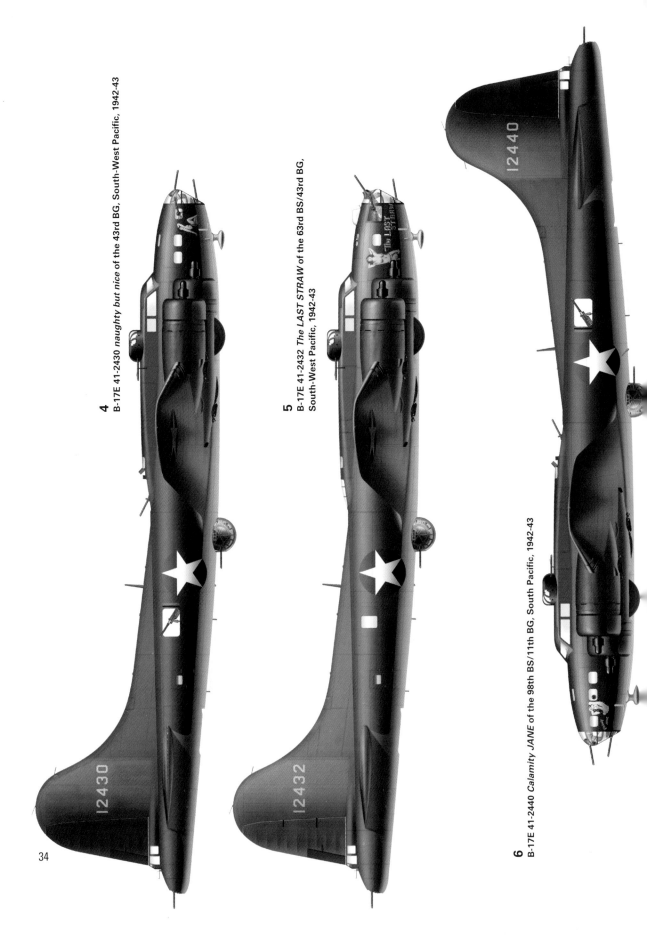

4

B-17E 41-2430 *naughty but nice* of the 43rd BG, South-West Pacific, 1942-43

5

B-17E 41-2432 *The LAST STRAW* of the 63rd BS/43rd BG,
South-West Pacific, 1942-43

6

B-17E 41-2440 *Calamity JANE* of the 98th BS/11th BG, South Pacific, 1942-43

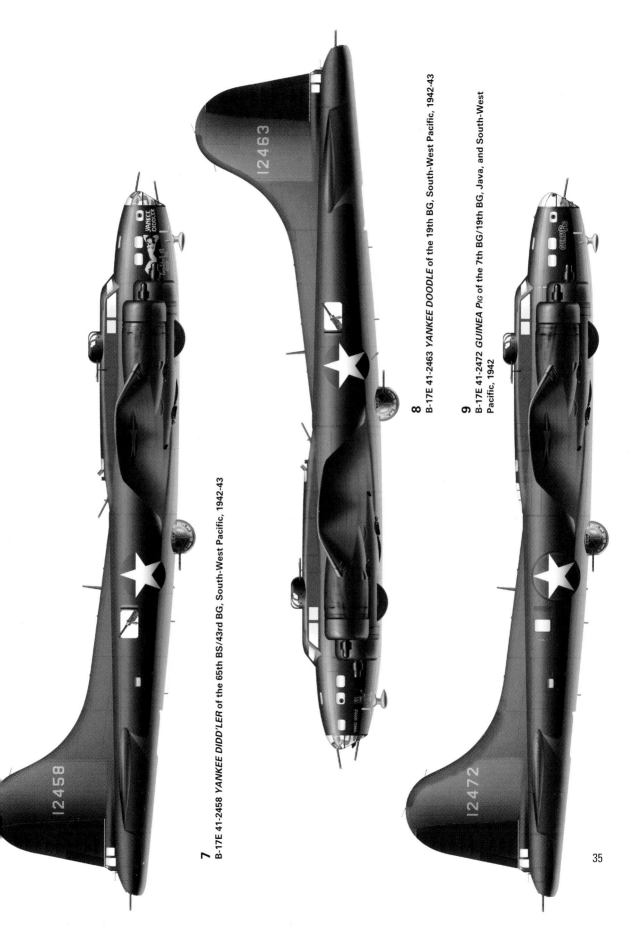

7
B-17E 41-2458 *YANKEE DIDD'LER* of the 65th BS/43rd BG, South-West Pacific, 1942-43

8
B-17E 41-2463 *YANKEE DOODLE* of the 19th BG, South-West Pacific, 1942-43

9
B-17E 41-2472 *GUINEA PIG* of the 7th BG/19th BG, Java, and South-West Pacific, 1942

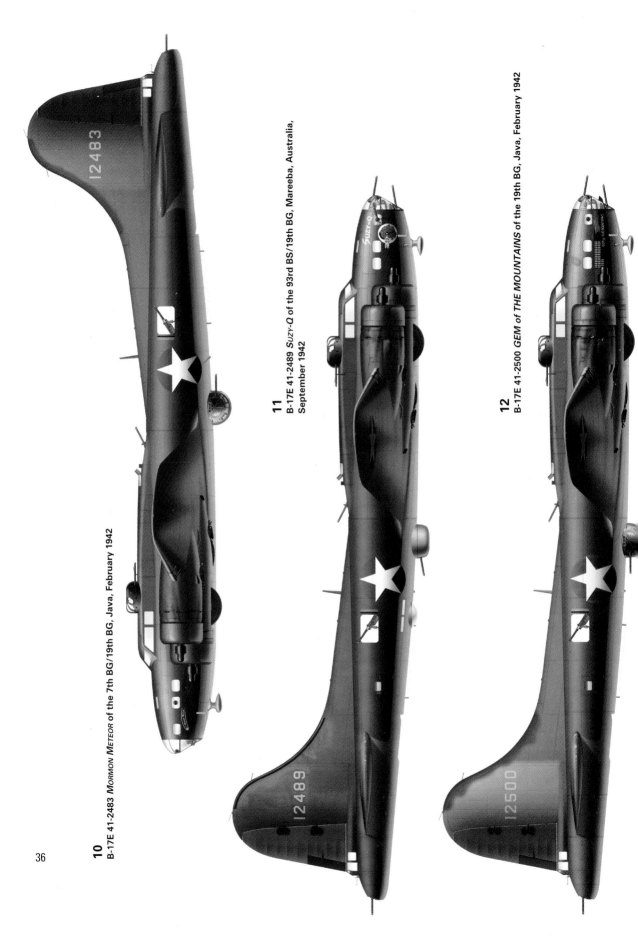

10
B-17E 41-2483 *MORMON METEOR* of the 7th BG/19th BG, Java, February 1942

11
B-17E 41-2489 *SUZY-Q* of the 93rd BS/19th BG, Mareeba, Australia,
September 1942

12
B-17E 41-2500 *GEM of THE MOUNTAINS* of the 19th BG, Java, February 1942

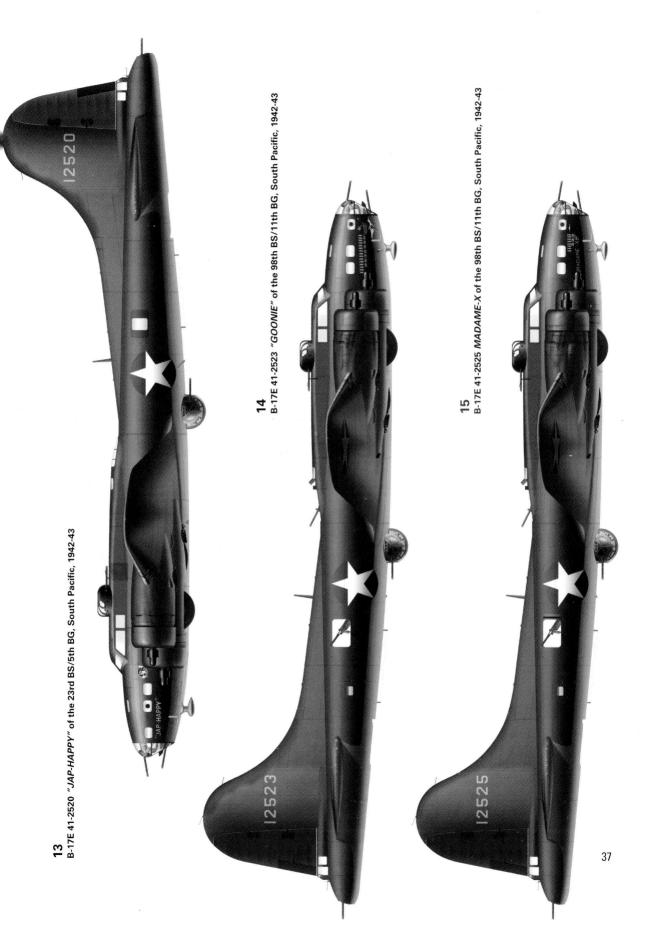

13
B-17E 41-2520 *"JAP-HAPPY"* of the 23rd BS/5th BG, South Pacific, 1942-43

14
B-17E 41-2523 *"GOONIE"* of the 98th BS/11th BG, South Pacific, 1942-43

15
B-17E 41-2525 *MADAME-X* of the 98th BS/11th BG, South Pacific, 1942-43

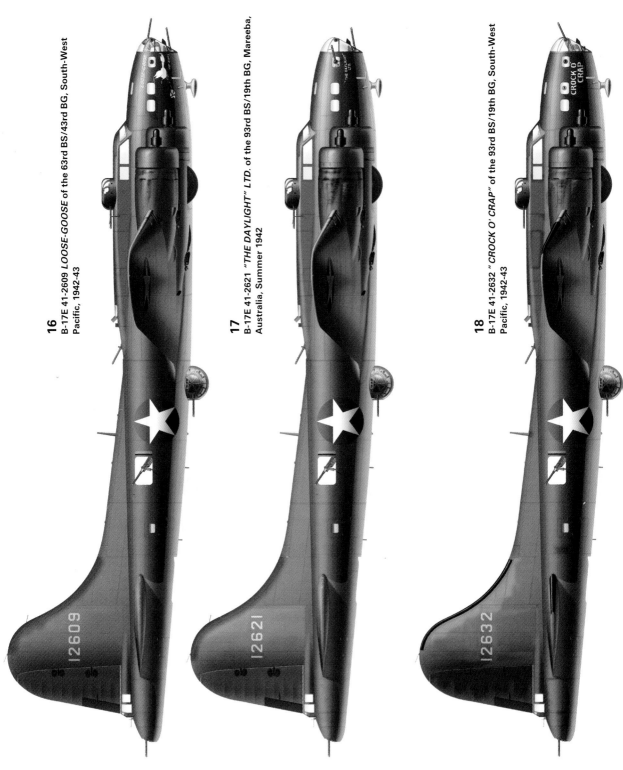

16
B-17E 41-2609 *LOOSE-GOOSE* of the 63rd BS/43rd BG, South-West
Pacific, 1942-43

17
B-17E 41-2621 *"THE DAYLIGHT" LTD.* of the 93rd BS/19th BG, Mareeba,
Australia, Summer 1942

18
B-17E 41-2632 *"CROCK O' CRAP"* of the 93rd BS/19th BG, South-West
Pacific, 1942-43

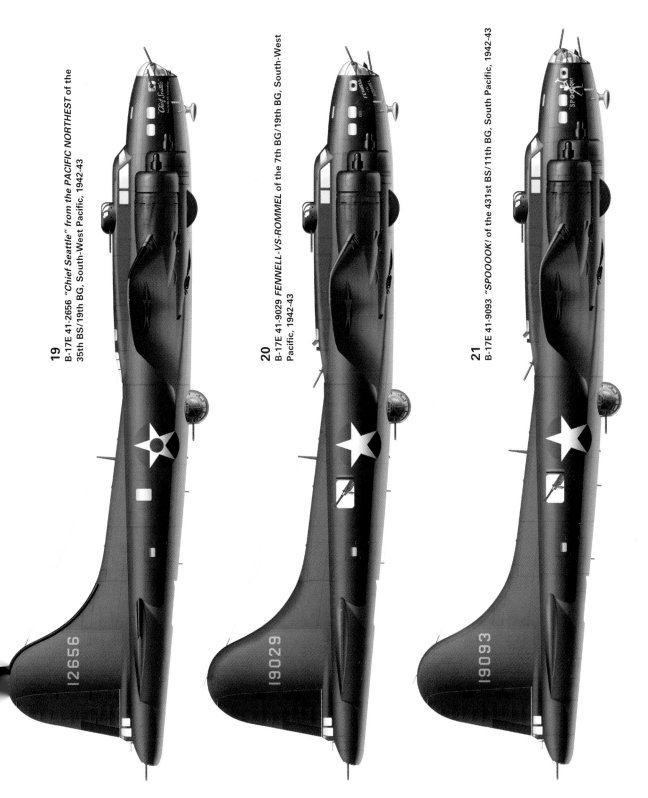

19
B-17E 41-2656 *"Chief Seattle" from the PACIFIC NORTHEST* of the
35th BS/19th BG, South-West Pacific, 1942-43

20
B-17E 41-9029 *FENNELL-VS-ROMMEL* of the 7th BG/19th BG, South-West
Pacific, 1942-43

21
B-17E 41-9093 *"SPOOOOK!* of the 431st BS/11th BG, South Pacific, 1942-43

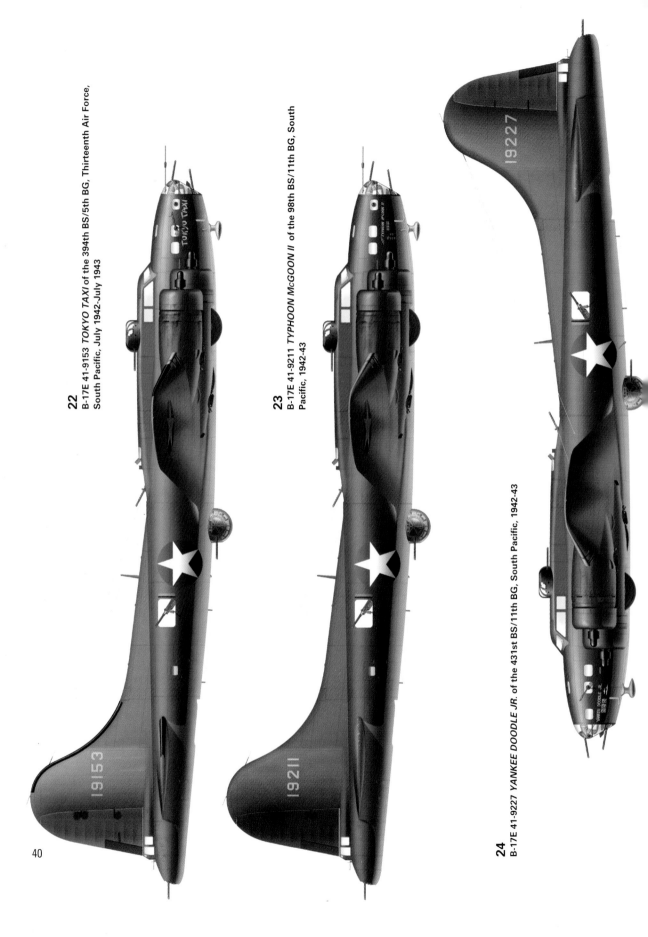

22
B-17E 41-9153 *TOKYO TAXI* of the 394th BS/5th BG, Thirteenth Air Force, South Pacific, July 1942-July 1943

23
B-17E 41-9211 *TYPHOON McGOON II* of the 98th BS/11th BG, South Pacific, 1942-43

24
B-17E 41-9227 *YANKEE DOODLE JR.* of the 431st BS/11th BG, South Pacific, 1942-43

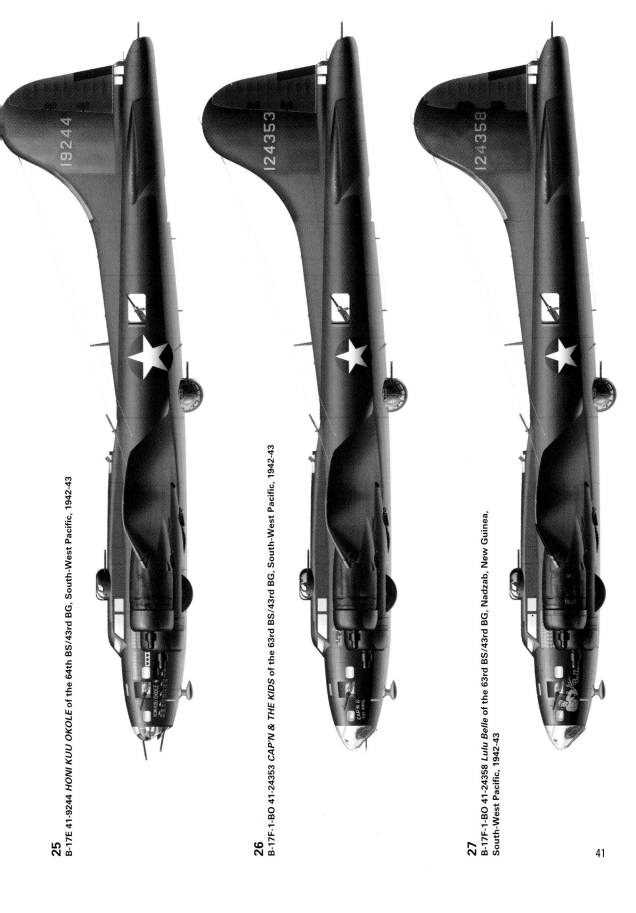

25
B-17E 41-9244 *HONI KUU OKOLE* of the 64th BS/43rd BG, South-West Pacific, 1942-43

26
B-17F-1-BO 41-24353 *CAP'N & THE KIDS* of the 63rd BS/43rd BG, South-West Pacific, 1942-43

27
B-17F-1-BO 41-24358 *Lulu Belle* of the 63rd BS/43rd BG, Nadzab, New Guinea, South-West Pacific, 1942-43

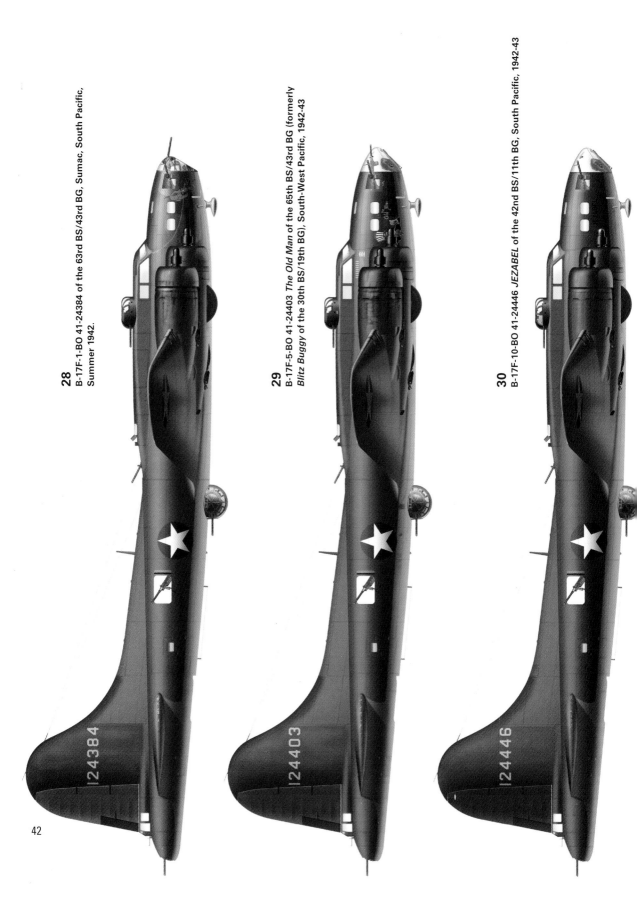

28
B-17F-1-BO 41-24384 of the 63rd BS/43rd BG, Sumac, South Pacific,
Summer 1942.

29
B-17F-5-BO 41-24403 *The Old Man* of the 65th BS/43rd BG (formerly
Blitz Buggy of the 30th BS/19th BG), South-West Pacific, 1942-43

30
B-17F-10-BO 41-24446 *JEZABEL* of the 42nd BS/11th BG, South Pacific, 1942-43

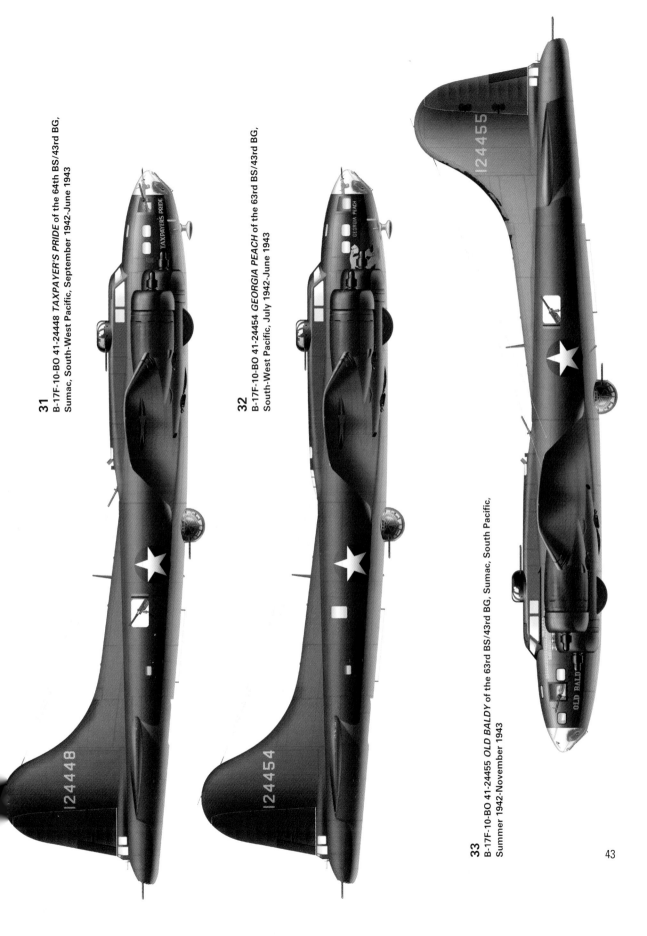

31
B-17F-10-BO 41-24448 *TAXPAYER'S PRIDE* of the 64th BS/43rd BG,
Sumac, South-West Pacific, September 1942-June 1943

32
B-17F-10-BO 41-24454 *GEORGIA PEACH* of the 63rd BS/43rd BG,
South-West Pacific, July 1942-June 1943

33
B-17F-10-BO 41-24455 *OLD BALDY* of the 63rd BS/43rd BG, Sumac, South Pacific,
Summer 1942-November 1943

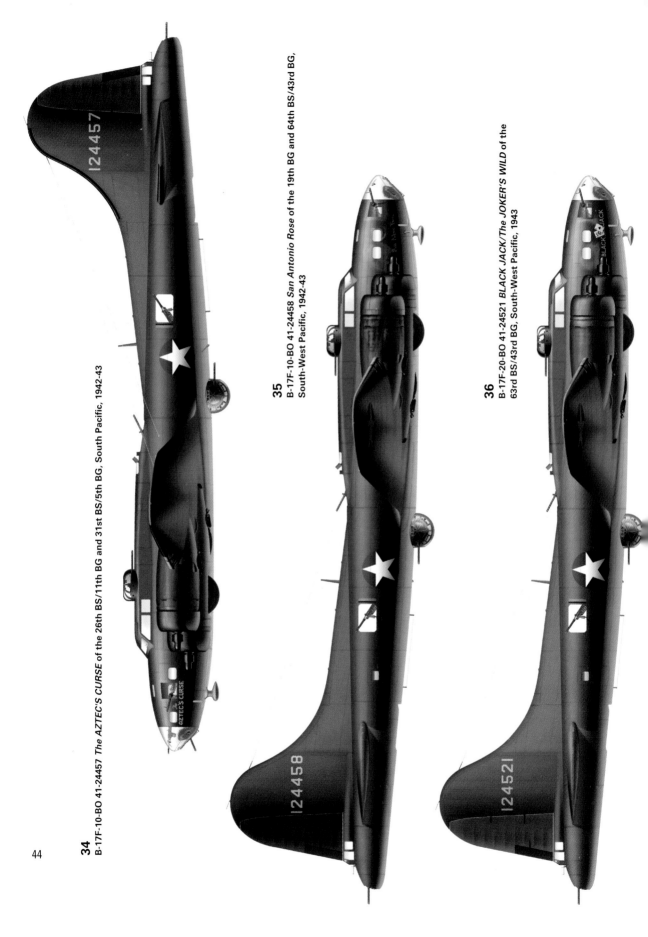

34
B-17F-10-BO 41-24457 *The AZTEC'S CURSE* of the 26th BS/11th BG and 31st BS/5th BG, South Pacific, 1942-43

35
B-17F-10-BO 41-24458 *San Antonio Rose* of the 19th BG and 64th BS/43rd BG, South-West Pacific, 1942-43

36
B-17F-20-BO 41-24521 *BLACK JACK/The JOKER'S WILD* of the 63rd BS/43rd BG, South-West Pacific, 1943

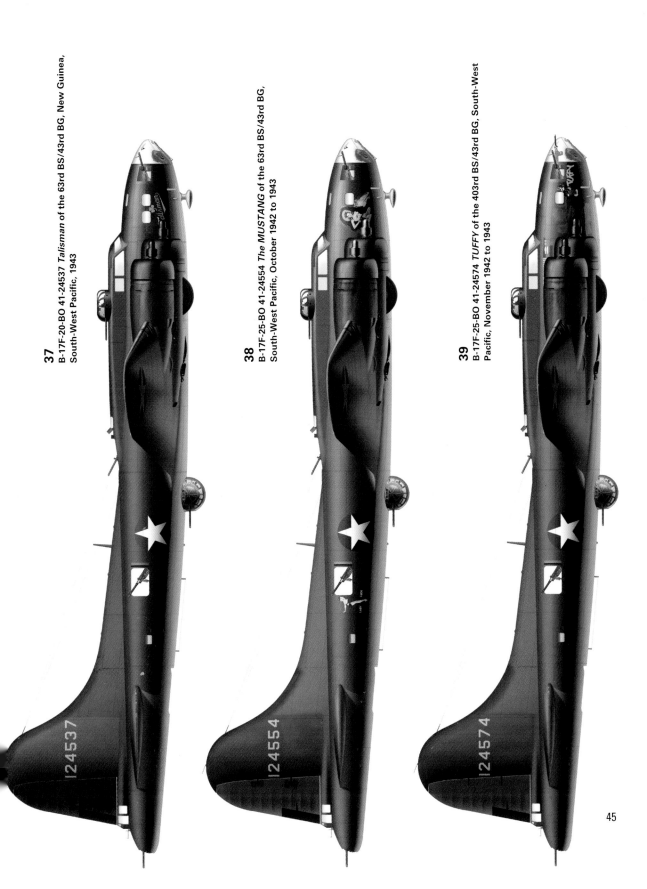

37
B-17F-20-BO 41-24537 *Talisman* of the 63rd BS/43rd BG, New Guinea, South-West Pacific, 1943

38
B-17F-25-BO 41-24554 *The MUSTANG* of the 63rd BS/43rd BG, South-West Pacific, October 1942 to 1943

39
B-17F-25-BO 41-24574 *TUFFY* of the 403rd BS/43rd BG, South-West Pacific, November 1942 to 1943

This nose art section has been specially created by profile artist Mark Styling so as to better illustrate the colourful artworks worn by the Flying Fortresses featured in profile within this volume. These drawings have been produced following exhaustive cross-referencing with published bomb group histories, correspondence with surviving veterans and their families and the detailed study of original photographs.

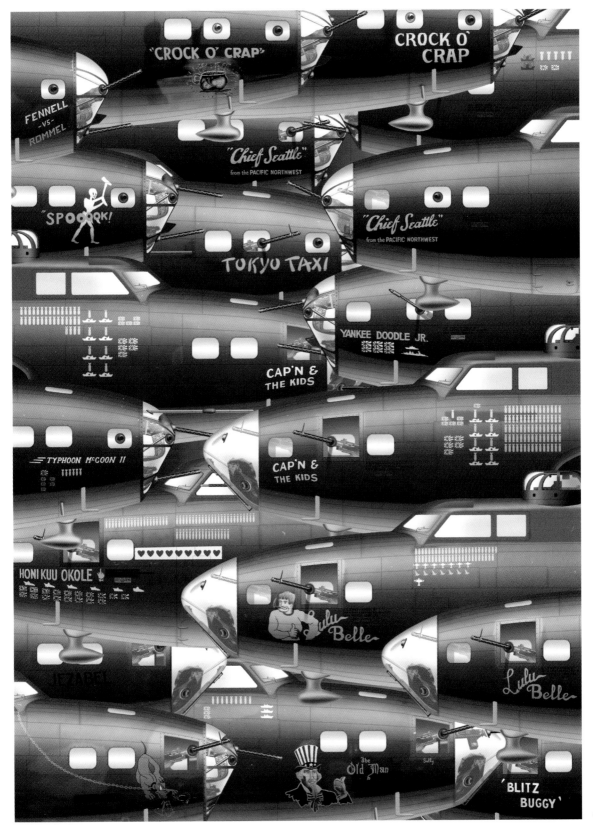

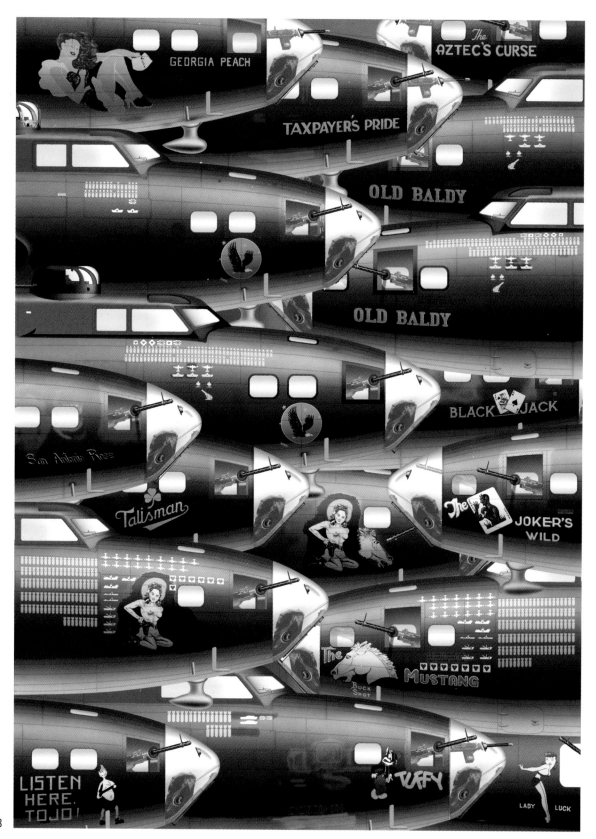

The 19th BG's B-17E 41-2633 *Sally* suffered this relatively minor accident on 27 June 1942 following a raid on the Japanese airfield at Lae. Capt Wilbur Beezley struck a barrier on the runway at the advance base at Mareeba in the dark and the impact blew out the left tyre. The Fortress then dropped with such force that the landing gear ploughed up through the No 2 engine (*USAF*)

B-17E 41-2489 *Suzy-Q* was one of the most famous Fortresses of the Pacific War. Delivered to MacDill on 4 January 1942 and assigned to the 93rd BS/19th BG on 7 February, the bomber took part in all the Pacific battles except Midway, and its gunners claimed no less than 26 Japanese aircraft destroyed (*USAF*)

B-17E 41-2462 *Tojo's Jinx* of the 93rd BS/19th BG is seen under armed guard at Longreach, in Queensland, in June 1942. This Fortress was delivered to Geiger Field on 22 December 1941 and assigned to the 19th BG in Java on 11 February 1942. Strafed at Port Moresby on Christmas Day 1942, the aircraft was repaired and renamed *Billy*. The veteran B-17 duly became a hack aircraft for Lt Gen Krueger of the 6th Army. It was finally written off on 3 June 1945 (*USAF*)

area and hit an airfield. Here, the Japs had a neat line of aircraft, and we marched our bombs up the lot! Then we went to Rabaul on a high-altitude day raid, staging through Port Moresby and landing back there afterwards to load up again. This time we went back to Rabaul at night, and low down. After bombing, Hardison came down to the deck so that Johnny Geckeler could shoot up anti-aircraft emplacements firing at Allied aircraft above us.

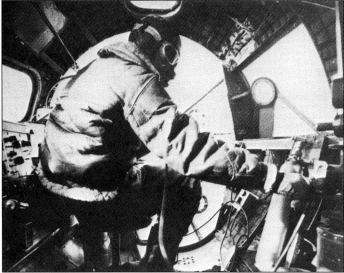

Also seen on the previous page, B-17E 41-2489 *Suzy-Q* of the 93rd BS/19th BG was named after the wife of its pilot, Maj Felix Hardison, CO of the 93rd BS. When the 19th BG retreated to Mareeba in September 1942, *Suzy-Q* was one of the proud remnants. The bomber eventually returned to the USA, arriving at Hamilton Field, California, on 12 July 1944, and finished its days at San Bernardino, before being scrapped sometime after July 1946 (*USAF*)

A bombardier is seen in the nose of a B-17E. Note the sockets in the nose cone and right cheek window for mounting a 0.30-cal machine gun (*USAF*)

Brig Gen Martin F Scanlon (second from right) gets a first-hand report from Lt R W Elliott on what happened to a Japanese fighter that attacked his Fortress over enemy territory (*USAF*)

'Back over Port Moresby, we ran into bad weather and the strip told us over the radio that we couldn't land because they were socked in all the way to 25,000 ft, so we had to go on to Horn Island. When we finally saw land we were so short of gas that Hardison had her running on only two throttled back engines, and we were losing altitude. We had missed Horn Island, for the land turned out to be the tip of the York Peninsula. The "Old Man" saw a clear spot in the trees and said he was going to set her down. He said, "I'm going to try and save the aeroplane, and you guys can get out now or ride on in with me". We all stayed.

'It was hard to see how he got *Suzy-Q* down in one piece with no damage, for when we got out we found the clearing was less than 1000 ft long and full of large melon holes. I had my picture taken in one of the latter that was between the main wheels, and it came up to my chest . . . and I'm over six feet tall!

'Our radioman finally got an SOS out, and after four days Australian Beauforts dropped food and equipment. Later, trucks brought us gas and the melon holes were filled for an attempt at flying

the *Suzy-Q* out. Guns and anything that could come out to
save weight were taken off and
Hardison had only a skeleton crew
aboard. He held her on the brakes
and gave her full power until the
tail pulled up and then let her roll.
About a third of the way down he
gave her one-third flaps and when
they reached the end of the strip
she was only doing 80, but they
made it.'

Femire flew no less than 92
missions in B-17s in the South-
West Pacific, and then went on to
complete 41 missions with the
Eighth Air Force in the ETO.
Finally, he flew 66 missions in
Invaders during the Korean War.

B-17E 41-2034 *TOJO'S PHYSIC* of
the 93rd BS/19th BG serves as the
backdrop for its crew, led by Capt
Felix M Hardison. This photograph
was taken at Longreach in June
1942. These men are, back row,
from left to right, Lt Albert Nice
(navigator), Lt Ellsworth McRoberts
(co-pilot), Capt Hardison, M/Sgt
David Semple (bombardier), S/Sgt
William Bestwick (engineer) and Cpl
William Koon (gunner). Kneeling,
from left to right, are Sgt Orville
Kiger (radio operator), unknown
(possibly *National Geographic*
writer Howell Walker) and Pte John
Irons (*USAF*)

The next major Pacific battle occurred on 3 June, when Japanese
forces attacked Midway Island. Eight B-17Es of the 431st BS/11th
BG, led by Lt Col Walter C Sweeney in *Knucklehead,* had arrived on
Midway from Hawaii on 29 May, and these were joined by nine more
the following day. The B-17Es (six returned to Oahu on 2 June) and
four B-26 medium bombers which were hurriedly converted to drop
torpedos, came under the command of Adm Chester W Nimitz,
Commander in Chief, Pacific. Nimitz flatly rejected a request by Maj
Gen Clarence L Tinker, Seventh Air Force Commander, that the
B-17Es be used to bomb Wake Island, a likely staging area for the
Japanese.

Tinker was finally able to bomb Wake on 6 June with the arrival of
four B-24s, which had a greater range than the B-17. The mission
proved to be an unmitigated disaster, and Tinker was lost when his
B-24 ran out of fuel and dived into the Pacific.

At 1230 hrs on 3 June, nine B-17Es left Midway in search of the
Japanese invasion fleet, which had been sighted by a PBY an hour
earlier only 700 miles away. At 1623 hrs the fleet of 26 ships was
spotted 570 miles from Midway. Six B-17Es of the 431st, along with
three B-17Es from the 31st BS/5th BG, attacked in three flights of
three from altitudes of 8000, 10,000 and 12,000 ft respectively.

This B-17E of the 72nd BS/5th BG
saw action from Midway in June
1942 (*USAF*)

ON WINGS WE CONQUER

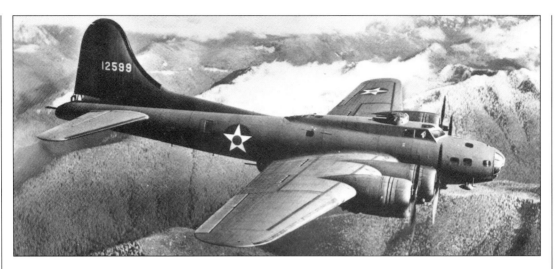

Sweeney and his two other B-17Es in the first flight picked out a large ship and tried to bomb it. Sweeney wrote;

'At the bomb-release line we encountered very heavy anti-aircraft fire. It continued throughout the attack and, as in the attacks that followed, was plenty heavy. My flight didn't claim any hits on this run – we hit all around the enemy but didn't see any evidence of damage.'

Capt Clement P Tokarz led the second element in *The Spider*. Sgt Horst Handrow, his tail gunner, remembered;

'There below was a task force that spread all over the Pacific. We didn't have enough gas to look any farther so we picked out the biggest battlewagon we could find and started to make a run on it with the bomb-bay doors open. The anti-aircraft fire was coming up now and the sky was black with it. Bang! We had a hit in the No 4 engine. On we went on our run. Bombs away. Two hits were scored with 500-lb bombs. The battleship seemed to blow up in one spot, and black smoke was coming out of her in a black cloud. She stopped right there, and the cans were coming in to aid the burning ship which couldn't go anywhere under its own power.'

The third element, led by Capt Cecil Faulkner, went after a cruiser and claimed to have hit it at the stem. One pilot in the second flight, Capt Paul Payne in *YANKEE DOODLE*, had two bombs hang up on the first trip so he made an additional individual run through the flak and claimed a direct hit and a near miss on a large transport, setting it on fire.

Sgt Handrow continued;

'As we left the area I could see another ship burning and a transport sinking. Not bad for nine Fortresses when it comes to attacking moving targets! The bombing mission was made at 10,000 ft. Home we came again, just dog-

B-17E 41-2599 was delivered to Lowry Modification Centre on 26 February 1942, before being assigned to the 93rd BS/19th BG. Named *Tugboat Annie,* this aircraft took part in the pivotal Battle of Midway in June 1942. Later that same year the bomber was transferred to the 65th BS/43rd BG, and it was ditched whilst still serving with this unit on 16 January 1943 (*Boeing*)

Field modifications to B-17E 41-2432 *The LAST STRAW*. Operated in turn by the 88th and 40th RSs (both 7th BG), the 28th BS/7th BG, the 19th BG and finally the 93rd BS/43rd BG, the bomber boasts an early attempt to improve the forward fire power of the Fortress in the Pacific by installing tail guns in the nose. This aircraft had arrived at Pearl Harbor on 7 December 1941, and it ended its days with the 443rd TCG (*USAF*)

B-17E 41-2432 *The LAST STRAW* is bombed up at Port Moresby in August 1942 whilst serving with the 19th BG (*USAF via Steve Birdsall*)

The crew of an unidentified B-17 strip down and clean their guns following a raid on New Guinea (*USAF*)

tired but happy. We had really done some good that day and we all remembered 7 December. We worked all that night loading bombs, gassing the ships and trying to get our No 4 engine in shape because we knew we would really need it the next day.'

Although the B-17 crews had claimed five hits, and Lt Ed Steedman and Capt Willard Woodbury near misses, they had been fooled by smoke screens laid down by destroyers, mistaking the smoke for burning ships.

That night seven more B-17Es from the 42nd BS/11th BG arrived at Midway to reinforce the small Fortress contingent. At 0415 hrs on 4 June, 14 B-17Es cleared Midway Island and assembled in the vicinity of Kure Island. Sweeney's crews then set out to attack the same main body that they had bombed the previous afternoon, but en route to the target word was received that another enemy task force, complete with carriers – namely *Soryu* and *Hiryu* – was approaching Midway and estimated to be only about 145 miles away. The B-17Es turned to intercept, climbing to 20,000 ft, but the carriers circled under broken cloud and the Fortress crews had to search for them.

Capt Payne spotted the first carrier, which was seen to break cloud cover – he directed the formation over his radio and went into the attack, followed by Capts Faulkner and Carl Wuertele in *Hel-En-Wings*. Lt Col Sweeney recalls;

'The enemy started firing as soon as we opened our bomb-bays. The fire wasn't effective, but it was a bit disturbing. The fighters came up to attack, manoeuvring beautifully, but they failed to follow through. It appeared that their heart was not in their work, and in no case was their attack pressed home. We divided our ships into three groups: each group was instructed to take a carrier, and we bombed away. We are fairly certain we hit the first carrier, but we didn't claim it. The second group, under the command of Capt Cecil Faulkner, hit its carrier amidships. Lt Col Brooke Allen, commanding the last flight, secured hits on the third carrier. We didn't have time to wait and see them sink, but we left knowing they were badly crippled.'

A B-17E waist gunner maintains a watchful eye during a photo-reconnaissance mission over New Guinea. The gun mount allowed him to swivel his 0.50-cal machine gun both inside and outside the window opening (*USAF*)

B-17E 41-2400 was built by Boeing and delivered to Douglas as the model for all B-17F production in California. Stripped of its Olive Drab camouflage, the Fortress was converted into a transport after many months of combat in the South Pacific, *Oklahoma Gal* having flown 203 bombing missions. It sank eight Japanese ships, and the bomber's gunners were credited with shooting down six enemy aircraft (*Douglas*)

In fact none of the enemy carriers was hit. Sgt Handrow, in Capt Tokarz's aircraft, wrote;

'We started our run, but couldn't get in because the clouds covered up the target and the anti-aircraft was thick. No 4 engine went out again, and we played around at 22,000 ft with the clouds and the anti-aircraft. Then we saw a big *Kago* carrier come out from under the clouds – the rising sun on it looked like a big bullseye, and we used it as such. Down went the bombs from three ships, the deck got three hits and the waterline four – she was sinking and burning at the same time. Zero fighters attacked us on the way home, but wouldn't come in close enough so we could get a good shot at them.

'We got a radio report that Midway was being bombed. What a funny feeling we got. What if we couldn't get in there? What the heck were we going to do? We didn't have enough gas to go back to Hawaii. As we drew closer we could see a cloud of black smoke hanging over the island. Something was really burning there, and our hopes sunk with that sight. In we came, and to give us a cheer we saw that the Marine ack-ack batteries had kept the runways open, even if everything else seemed to be hit.

'We landed and started to gas up and load bombs again for another run in the late afternoon at the Japs, who by then were only 90 miles away. Up again, and this time we picked out a big cruiser – but just as we started on the run, six Navy dive-bombers dived down on him. At last we were getting help from the Navy. So we picked out a nice transport loaded with Japs. Two hits and the Japs were swimming back to Japan. Home we went again, still fooling around with No 4 out – then No 2 started giving us trouble. It looked like our little fun picnic was over, because we were ordered back to Hawaii. Take-off from Midway was made at 0200 hrs. It was a tired crew that landed at Hickam that night. All the men in the crew got the Silver Star for this battle.'

Other B-17Es carried on the attack on 5 June. In the morning, eight B-17Es attacked a task force 130 miles from Midway, and claimed hits on two large warships. During the afternoon, six B-17Es claimed hits on a heavy cruiser 300 miles from Midway. The last strike by Seventh Air Force aircraft in the Battle of Midway was by five B-17Es, which bombed a heavy cruiser 425 miles from Midway.

One B-17E was shot down at sea 15 miles off the island – all except one of the crew were rescued. Another B-17E was lost due to fuel shortage.

The battle ended in victory for the US. Losses in aircraft and ships were heavy, but the Japanese had lost four valuable aircraft carriers. Between 3 and 5 June the B-17Es had flown 16 attacks (55 sorties) for the loss of two aircraft, and dropped 300 bombs, but they failed to register a single hit. This demonstrated that the strategic

B-17F 41-24448 *TAXPAYER'S PRIDE* joined the 28th BS/19th BG on 1 September 1942 and was shot down on 7 January 1943 (*Frank Hohmann*)

B-17E 41-2417 *MONKEY BIZZ-NESS* flew with the 63rd BS/43rd BG. Delivered to the Salt Lake City air depot on 19 January 1941 and assigned to the 19th BG in Hawaii just days later, this aircraft was sent to Java on 19 February 1942. It crashed in Queensland on 6 July 1942 when being piloted by Lt William Thompson and was salvaged (*www.aerothentic.com*)

B-17E 41-2621 *"THE DAYLIGHT" LTD.* of the 93rd BS/19th BG is seen after Lt Casper crash-landed at Mareeba on 26 August 1942. A relative newcomer to the South-West Pacific, having only been assigned to the 19th BG in Hawaii on 8 July 1942, 41-2621 was so badly damaged in the accident that it was written off (*USAF via Bill Cleveland*)

bomber, using conventional high-altitude tactics, posed little threat to warships under way. There were exceptions. On 25 August 1942, during the Battle of the Eastern Solomons, the Japanese credited a flight of B-17s with surprising the destroyer *Mutsuki* and sending it to the bottom when it stopped to take off troops from a sinking transport.

To divert attention away from Midway, and also to extend their defensive perimeter, the Japanese attacked the Aleutian Islands with an invasion force that included two aircraft carriers. Brig Gen William O Butler's Eleventh Air Force came under the control of the US Navy, and Army airmen were incorporated to defend Alaska. On 3 and 4 June 1942 the Japanese aircraft took off from their carriers and a break in the weather enabled Butler's B-17s and B-26s to attack the enemy vessels. However, no damage was inflicted.

In the wake of the Battle of Midway, a great shake-up of commands took place. Then on 4 August Maj Gen George C Kenney was officially placed in charge of MacArthur's air operations in the South-West Pacific, taking command of the Allied Air Forces. On 7 August Kenney asked Washington for authorisation to form the Fifth Air

Force, and this was received two days later. He appointed Brig Gen Kenneth N Walker as commander of V Bomber Command – Walker had been one of 'Hap' Arnold's staff officers at AWPD. One of Kenney's first tasks was to clear the skies of Japanese aircraft over New Guinea and then New Britain, and to advance on the Admiralty Islands.

Between 7 and 12 August, the 19th BG attacked targets near Rabaul, and was awarded a second Distinguished Unit Cross (DUC) for these missions. For his actions on 6-7 August, Capt Harl Pease Jr of the 93rd BS/19th BG was

posthumously awarded the Medal of Honor. On the 6th Pease was forced to return to Mareeba from a reconnaissance mission over New Britain when an engine failed. He was anxious to take part in the big raid planned for the following day against Vunakanau airfield, – a large airstrip 500 miles north of New Britain, in the Bismarck Archipelago. He and his crew worked for hours on B-17E 41-2429 to rectify its engine problem. They finally arrived at Port Moresby after midnight, where they borrowed a hand pump from the crew of Maj Hardison's *SUZY-Q* because their bad engine had no electric fuel pump.

On the morning of 7 August, 16 B-17s of the 19th BG, led by Lt Col Carmichael, took off for Vunakanau airfield, where 150 bombers threatened the US Marine Corps' landings on Guadalcanal. One B-17 crashed on take-off and two aborted with mechanical malfunctions, but by skilful flying, Pease maintained his position in the formation, despite a still troublesome engine, and made it to the target.

At this point the bad engine gave out. Pease feathered it and dropped his bombs on the target, but the Japanese fighters soon singled out his crippled B-17. In the air battle that continued after the bombers left the target, Pease's Fortress was hit in the bomb-bay tank, which burst into flames, and the bomber fell behind the formation and was lost. There were reports of two parachutes being seen, and some years later it emerged that Pease and Sgt Czehowski, a gunner, did bale out and were taken prisoner. On 8 October 1942 the Japanese at Rabaul summarily executed Pease, Czehowski and four other prisoners.

Members of the salvage team assigned to retrieve *"THE DAYLIGHT" LTD.* take a break from their work to pose for the camera. Built by Boeing in early 1942 and delivered to the Lowry Modification Center in Colorado on 14 March, 41-2621 had been based at Boise, Idaho, from 1 April until assigned to the 93rd BS/19th BG in Hawaii on 8 July. Being such a new airframe, the bomber no doubt yielded many spare parts for fellow B-17Es at Mareeba (*www.aerothentic.com*)

A B-17E of the 19th BG sits in a camouflage netting-covered blister hangar at Mareeba in the summer of 1942 (USAF)

Top
19th BG personnel parade in front of B-17E 41-2462 *Tojo's Jinx* **at Mareeba in late 1942 (***USAF***)**

Above
This unidentified B-17E, which survived more than 200 combat missions, is seen at Hickam Field, Hawaii, in late 1943 (*USAF***)**

B-17E 41-2656 "C*hief Seattle" from the PACIFIC NORTHWEST* **was assigned to the 435th BS/19th BG on 29 May 1942. It was lost on a recce mission on 19 August 1942 (***Boeing***)**

Capt Harl Pease was typical of the men that flew the early B-17 missions against the Japanese in the South-West Pacific. Another was engineer Sgt Frank Hohmann, who survived his long tour in combat with the 19th BG. He remembers;

'Until 15 November 1942, when the 19th BG was sent back to the States, all flights out over the Coral Sea or to Port Moresby were counted as combat missions. We endured 110 Jap bombing raids whilst based in Port Moresby during this time frame. We had flown almost every day with the 19th because there was a shortage of aeroplanes and even crews to man them. When the 43rd BG took over from the 19th early in November, we were transferred to this group. They brought their own crews and only a small number of aeroplanes, which they had first seen upon arriving in Australia.'

'KEN'S MEN'

The 43rd BG had arrived in the South-West Pacific in March 1942 to become a part of the Fifth Air Force, the group initially operating from bases in Australia before moving to Port Moresby on 14 September 1942. During October several daylight and night raids were made on Rabaul, the main Japanese base in the Pacific, as pilot Jim Dieffenderfer recalls;

'We had few B-17s early on. Daylight flights were two-ship "buddy flights", mostly low-level reconnaissance. Single aircraft flights were used for long-range reconnaissance, usually at high altitude. At night we would make skip-bombing attacks on Japanese ships.'

B-17F 41-24520 *Fightin' Swede* **and another 63rd BS/43rd BG B-17 are seen after skip-bombing practice against the hulk of the SS** *Pruth* **(just visible on the horizon above the second Fortress) in Port Moresby harbour. Assigned to the 19th BG on 1 September 1942 and transferred to the 43rd BG in November of that year, 41-24520 was shot down on 11 May 1943** (*Roger Vargas via Steve Birdsall*)

Crews would fly as low as 250 ft along the moon slick on top of the water before releasing their bombs 100 ft short of the target, 'skipping' their ordnance off the water into the side of the Japanese vessels at the waterline. Dieffenderfer continues;

'To hit a ship from high altitude you need a large formation. We tried as low as 3500 ft with a single aircraft without result. All the surface ship captain needed was field glasses, and when he saw the bombs leave the bomb-bay he would call for hard aport or starboard and we would miss, so all B-17 skip-bombing was done at night. We were the only ones with the range to go to Rabaul. The B-25 skip-bombed in the daytime during the Battle of the Bismarck Sea, but they had us in B-17s spaced above the convoy 3500 to 7500 ft. To get everyone looking up as soon as we bombed, Beaufighters with 20 mm cannons in the nose followed by B-25s with 0.50-cals in the nose came in strafing and skip-bombing.

'Our procedure was to approach a harbour at 2000-4000 ft, locate the ship, cut throttles and glide down over land, getting below the line of sight of the ship and the mountains so you were not silhouetted against the sky. Come out off the land toward the target at 250 mph

Lt Jim Dieffenderfer poses in the cockpit of his battle-weary B-17F 41-24455 *OLD BALDY*. **The bomber boasts a most impressive scoreboard** (*Jim Dieffenderfer*)

and 250 ft altitude, your airspeed starts falling off as soon as you level off. We didn't want it below 200 mph when bombs were toggled out one at a time by the bombardier, so full throttle was applied when 200 mph was reached, or when you were over the ship, whichever came first. The noise from this, plus the bombs going off, must have caused much confusion to the gunners on the ship, because just before getting to the vessel they started firing and there was little to no flak after passing over it.

'A slow turn for evasion and observation was the accepted departure, then a course for home and a climb for altitude. It sounds a lot easier than it is. Distances and altitudes are difficult to judge at night. All of this was done in conjunction with other aircraft so as to keep the enemy looking up. I don't believe a lone aircraft would have survived going into a harbour at such a low altitude.'

Skip-bombing was dangerous but devastatingly effective. One of the group's pioneers in its development was Capt Kenneth D McCullar, a flamboyant gambler and a fearless and aggressive pilot who flew B-17F 41-24521 *BLACK JACK* with the 63rd BS/43rd BG. In September 1942, when McCullar had picked out the new Fortress, he had noted the last two digits of its serial and had the name and two playing cards (a 'Jack' and an 'ace') painted on the nose by Sgt Ernie Vandal.

The B-17F was the first Fortress model to enter really large-scale output, following on from 512 B-17Es – the final 300 E-models were duly converted to B-17Fs. The most notable difference between the two models was the frameless Plexiglas nose cone of the B-17F, which gave the bombardier better all-round visibility, and was fitted with duplicate sockets for a single 0.30-cal gun to fire from the upper quarter or lower right areas of the nose. However, it was too weak to support a 0.50-cal machine gun, and field engineers had to strengthen it.

McCullar had Sgt Tony DeAngelis and his groundcrew install a fixed 0.50-cal machine gun in the nose, with a firing button on the pilot's control wheel, so that he could blast away at enemy ships and help deter head-on attacks by fighters.

Problems with the bombardier and navigator getting in each other's way when the guns were fired were eased slightly with the B-17F by enlarging and staggering the side nose gun windows. USAAF modification centres also bulged the side windows outward to permit the nose gunners a wider forward-firing sweep. These bulged nose guns, known as 'cheek' guns, eventually became standard.

BLACK JACK and Ken McCullar became legendary. Flying as many as three combat missions in one day, they always came back, sometimes against the odds. On the night of 24 November 1942, the 43rd BG was sent to bomb five troop-laden Japanese destroyers heading from

B-17E 41-2458 *YANKEE DIDD'LER* of the 65th BS/43rd BG, which was sent to the 317th Troop Carrier Group (TCG) at Dobodura in November 1943, and was written off on 27 January 1945 (*www.aerothentic.com*)

B-17F 41-24550 of the 403rd BS/43rd BG was ditched by Lt Ealon Hocutt in Bootless Inlet, Port Moresby, on 14 December 1942 after losing two engines on take-off (*US Army via Steve Birdsall*)

An aerial view of B-17s from the 43rd BG parked in their revetments at Seven Mile airfield, Port Moresby. By August 1942, the Queensland-based 43rd BG had become the fifth B-17 group to be deployed against Japan, and this unit was later awarded a Distinguished Unit Citation for skip-bombing shipping in the South Pacific, including attacks on enemy vessels during the Battle of the Bismarck Sea on 2-4 March 1943 (*USAF*)

Lt Harry Staley's crew from the 63rd BS/43rd BG pose in front of B-17F 41-24521 *BLACK JACK* after flying their last mission, on 14 February 1943. Whilst over Rabaul a shell had torn through the No 3 supercharger and nacelle. The fixed machine gun in the lower nose was fitted for the B-17's original pilot, Lt Ken McCullar (*Harry Staley via Steve Birdsall*)

Rabaul into the Huon Gulf. McCullar picked out the *Hayashio* and made the first of his five bombing runs at just 200 ft amid heavy tracer fire. His bombs hit just off the rear of the destroyer but the Japanese gunners had set off ammunition in *BLACK JACK's* tail section, starting a fire. The crew extinguished the flames as McCullar positioned the B-17 for another bomb run.

BLACK JACK took more hits, and shell fragments wounded three of the crew, but McCullar got his bombs away and the explosions started a blaze in the bow of the vessel. Japanese destroyers could put up a devastating shield of fire, and *BLACK JACK* was badly hit when McCullar made his third attack. The port outboard engine was hit and the controls shot away, but this did not prevent him attempting a fourth bomb run.

His bombs rocked the *Hayashio* but *BLACK JACK* received yet more damage. With two bombs remaining, McCullar carried out his fifth and final attack, this time from 400 ft. Now the inboard engine on the starboard wing was also hit and the fuel system was ruptured. With only two good engines, *BLACK JACK* began losing altitude.

The aircraft and crew were faced with a long climb back over the Owen Stanley Mountains, which rise to a height of two miles, back to Port Moresby. The port engine could have burst into flames or exploded at any time, McCullar clearly able to see it glowing cherry red in the darkness. Finally, the propeller unit ground itself loose from the engine and spun off into the night. The engine cooled down but the stricken B-17 was sinking alarmingly and the crew threw out their ammunition and loose equipment to lighten it. The pilots tried to restart the other damaged engine and were finally able to get partial power from it.

Slowly, *BLACK JACK* began climbing, but it took an agonising two-and-a-half hours to reach 10,000 ft – just enough height for the Fortress to make it safely through a mountain pass, and for McCullar to set the B-17 down safely on the ground at Port Moresby's Seven Mile strip. An RAAF Beaufort was sent to finish off the *Hayashio*, but as the bomber began its run the enemy destroyer exploded and sank.

BLACK JACK was out of action for two months while it was repaired, and during that time

The port side of B-17F 41-24521 *BLACK JACK* featured the name *The JOKER'S WILD*, this artwork being added by the Staley crew after they had taken over the Fortress from Ken McCullar (*Harry Staley via Steve Birdsall*)

McCullar took command of the 64th BS. His co-pilot, Lt Harry Staley, took over *Black Jack,* whose port side was adorned with the name *The JOKER'S WILD*, complete with a devil's playing card. Staley's crew flew five missions in 41-24521 before the Fortress was badly shot up over Rabaul on 14 February 1943. Staley and his men subsequently went on to complete their tour in other aircraft.

McCullar was killed on 15 April 1943 when 64th BS B-17E 41-9209 *Blues in the Nite* hit a wallaby during a night take-off from Seven Mile airfield. There were also reports that there may have been an engine fire before the aircraft hit the animal. After the accident the 43rd BG called itself 'Ken's Men' in honour of Kenneth D McCullar.

Meanwhile, late in 1942, indications were that the Japanese were getting ready to despatch a large expeditionary force to relieve their garrisons at Lae and Salamaua, on the Huon Gulf of New Guinea. Certainly the build-up in shipping in Rabaul Harbour proved as much. By early January 1943 more than 90 vessels were moored there, and Maj Gen Kenney ordered a maximum effort at dawn on the 5th.

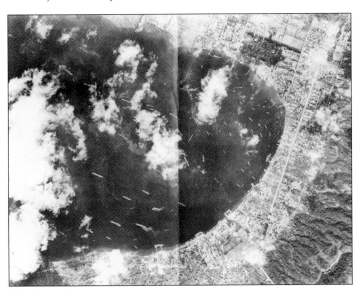

This high altitude view of Rabaul Harbour was taken in early 1943 by a 63rd BS B-17 crew on a reconnaissance mission. Squadron pilot Jim Dieffenderfer recalls;

'The Japanese didn't have any bright searchlights in-theatre until after Singapore fell. They must have brought all the searchlights to Rabaul, for they surprised us one night. We came in as usual at an altitude of about 7000 ft and they blinded us. We had to go on instruments to fly the aeroplane. I put it into a steep dive and held it for around one minute (seemed like an hour). Then I pulled up and out – i.e. turned to the left and got out of the beam. Ack-ack was pretty intense when in the beam, but not as bad before the lights came. In fact, the flak was sometimes helpful. Our navigation was by dead reckoning or the stars, and sometimes we would not have found the target unless they shot ack-ack at us. Our procedure was to navigate to where we thought the target was, and if overcast, circle a few times. If we were not fired upon we would continue on for another ten minutes and circle again. Do this several times and sure enough we would get fired upon, then we could get below the clouds, orient ourselves and find our target.'

A final thought on night bombing Rabaul comes from Frank Hohmann of the 28th BS/19th BG;

'We had a new man bale out over Rabaul (60,000 Japanese for company) when the pilot put the aircraft in a steep dive to escape the lights and AA' (*Jim Dieffenderfer*)

Brig Gen Kenneth N Walker, commanding general of V Bomber Command, did not want his B-17s and B-24s to take off from Port Moresby in darkness because of the difficulty in getting into formation, and wanted instead to strike at Rabaul Harbour at noon. But Kenney was prepared to risk a strung-out formation because he knew Japanese fighters would not be airborne in the early hours, whereas at noon they would be up in force.

Disobeying specific orders from Kenney himself, Walker moved the take-off time for a noon attack, and decided to fly on the mission as an observer aboard B-17F 41-24458 *San Antonio Rose*, piloted by 64th BS CO Maj Allen Lindberg. Fred Wesche, one of the B-17 pilots involved in this mission, later wrote;

'I was on what most of us thought was a suicide mission. When it was announced that it was going to be done in broad daylight at noontime, at low altitude – something like 5000 ft – over the most heavily defended target in the Pacific, most of us went away shaking our heads. Many of us believed we wouldn't come back from it.'

The formation of six B-17s from the 43rd BG and six B-24s from the 90th BG reached Rabaul, and at noon bombed the shipping there. Ten vessels were hit, the *Kurapaku Maru* being sunk and six others set on fire. However, flak was heavy and the fighters (both Army 'Oscars' and Navy Zeros) were many and determined. Fred Wesche, who was flying on the wing of *San Antonio Rose* over Rabaul, recalls;

'We went over the target and all of us got attacked. I was shot up. Nobody was injured, fortunately, but the aeroplane was kind of banged up a little bit. We had to break formation over the target to bomb individually and then we were supposed to form up immediately after crossing the target. But no sooner had we dropped our bombs than my tail gunner said, "Hey, there's somebody in trouble behind us". So we made a turn and looked back, and there was an aeroplane, one of our aeroplanes, going down, smoking and on fire – not necessarily fire, but smoke anyway – headed down obviously for a cloud bank, with a whole cloud of fighters on top of him. There must have been 15 or 20 fighters. Of course they gang up on a cripple, you know, polish that one off with no trouble, but he disappeared into a cloud bank and we never saw him again. It turns out it was the general. Gen Walker was on board.'

Kenney ordered all available reconnaissance aircraft to search for survivors, and that evening a B-17 was seen on a coral reef in the Trobriand Islands. A Catalina rescued the crew but it was not Lindberg's. Walker was posthumously awarded the Medal of Honor.

In all, Rabaul was bombed 13 times in January 1943, but never by more than 12 aircraft. At this time, of the 55 B-17E/Fs in the 43rd BG, about 20 were usually under repair or maintenance, leaving 12-14 B-17s available for raids, while the best the B-24s could muster was about 15 Liberators from 60 in theatre.

On 8 January Capt Jay Rousek's 65th BS crew flew a mission to Salama/Lae, on the north coast of New Guinea, in B-17E 41-2657 *Old Faithful,* as engineer Sgt Hohmann recalls;

'We had just cleared the Owen Stanley Range and were about to form up into a compact group when we were attacked by 12 Zeros.

The crew was able to drive them off when one aeroplane came out of nowhere at "12 o'clock high". He was way out of the range of my 0.50-cals but I fired off a round or two to let him know that I saw him. In return, I saw his two wing guns wink red while in a dive upside down. That's all I saw, and he pulled up out of the dive going away from me.

'I felt Jay pull on my flight suit and I tried to tell him what I saw and why I was so frustrated when he told me to go below to see what damage we had sustained. That's when I knew we were hit. I dropped down into the navigator/bombardier's position and found Walt Lucien, the bombardier, in tears and pointing towards Duffee, the navigator.

'One look told me that Lt Roy K Duffee was dead. He was leaning forward on the table just as I had seen him many times, only this time the whole top and back of his head was caved in. I took his pulse and confirmed that he was dead, and I took him out of his chair, laid him on the floor and covered him with his flight jacket. I asked Walt if he was hurt. He shook his head but I gave him a shot of morphine, then went back to tell Rousek what had happened.

'I found Leaman on the flight deck trying to unbuckle the co-pilot from his seat. That's when I realised that the co-pilot was hit. Doug and I finally got 2Lt Eugene 'Dutch' Benedetti on the floor and found that he had lost the whole right side of his face and head. We gave him a shot of morphine and laid him on the now closed door to the navigator's compartment.

'Jay Rousek was bleeding through his trousers. I asked him if he was all right and did he need a shot. "No", he said. Then he told me to take the right seat just in case. Way back, when we were flying to the Galapagos Islands, Jay let me sit in the left seat and one day had the bright idea of letting me learn to land the aeroplane from that seat. I made ten landings with him in the right seat after that, never thinking it would come in handy.

'I made Leaman, the engineer, stand astride Benedetti to watch the needles and the controls that I normally did – he never forgave me for this. This was Benedetti's second mission with us, our original co-pilot, Lt Vern Strawser, having taken command of his own crew as pilot (Benedetti went home and later became a university professor and ran in 20 marathons, winning in his weight class 18 times all over the world – author). Strawser was killed on his fourth mission in a frontal attack by a Zero.

'Jay had already turned around and was climbing to clear the Owen Stanleys. We landed safely, with me using the brakes. It was on the ground that I found out that Jay had been hit in the legs. The doctors gave us a look, a day off and time for me to think why I couldn't hit

Capt Jay P Rousek's crew of B-17F 41-24448 *Taxpayer's Pride* from the 28th BS/19th BG. They are, in the back row from left to right, 2Lt Walt J Lucien (bombardier), 1Lt Roy K Duffee (navigator, killed in action over Salamua on 8 January 1943), 2Lt Vernon A Strawser (co-pilot, killed in action in February 1943) and Capt Jay P Rousek (pilot). Kneeling, from left to right, are Pte Ralph H Thomas (assistant engineer, missing in action over Rabaul on 26 June 1943), Sgt Alex D Leaman (tail gunner), Sgt S N Mills (radio operator), Sgt Frank P Hohmann (engineer) and Pte F E McGlothlin (assistant radio operator). *Taxpayer's Pride* crashed near Rabaul on 26 June 1943 (*Frank Hohmann*)

that Jap. That's when I discovered that the Jap 20 mm wing guns had a greater range than my 0.50-cal guns.

'After returning from R&R, the bombardier was assigned to another crew. However, the trauma of seeing a close friend killed from a 20 mm shell exploding just inches above the back of his head was too much, and he fell to pieces on the first mission with this crew and never flew again.'

When the Japanese on Rabaul sent a convoy of 15 to 20 ships to land 7000 troops of the LI (51st) Infantry Division at Lae on 1 March 1943, every available US bomber was made ready. The Battle of the Bismarck Sea was about the commence. Seven B-17s sent to bomb the convoy late in the evening dropped flares and flew over the Bismarck Sea at 50 ft with their lights on to attract fire, but they failed to find any enemy vessels along the north coast of New Britain.

The following day Lt Herbert Derr and his crew in *Dumbo* flew a 'shadow recon' mission of more than 11 hours, reporting the movement of the Japanese convoy and giving weather reports. Early on the morning of the 2nd eight B-17s from the 63rd BS/43rd BG, flying in loose formation and led by Maj Edward W Scott Jr in *Talisman,* carried out the first strike on the convoy.

Scott and his two wingmen, Capt Harry Staley on his right and Lt Francis Denault in *Lulu Belle* on his left, attacked a large transport from 6500 ft. The B-17s, which had failed to link up with their P-38 fighter escorts, were immediately attacked by eight Zeros. They attacked from high and low altitude, but none of the bombers was shot down and the bombs found their mark. The large transport, which happened to be the command ship of the LI Division, disappeared in a plume of smoke and flame and was destroyed by a series of explosions. Lt Jim Murphy, pilot of B-17F 41-24381 *PANAMA HATTIE,* singled out a destroyer, but his first bomb salvo missed. He tried again, although the return fire was so intense that he switched his attention to a freighter. His bombardier released a bomb and the vessel split in two.

A second flight of 20 B-17s arrived and claimed two hits and four near misses on the convoy. That evening 11 Fortresses carried out the third and final attack of the day. One more vessel was claimed sunk. That night the convoy was shadowed from the air, and on the morning of the 3rd the B-17s, this time escorted by P-38s, attacked again.

About 15 enemy fighters singled out *PANAMA HATTIE*, piloted on this occasion by Lt William M Thompson, and the B-17F gunners claimed three fighters shot down. *Ka-Puhio-Wela,* flown by Lt Woodrow Moore, was attacked from below by an A6M3 'Hamp'. A fire broke out in the radio room and Moore pulled up and away from his wingman, B-17F 41-24358 *Lulu Belle,* flown by Lt Denault, and salvoed his bombs – the doomed B-17 disintegrated before hitting the sea, seven men being seen to bale out. One crewman fell out of his harness and Japanese fighters strafed the others as they descended.

Another bomber singled out for attention by the fighters was B-17F 41-24455 *OLD BALDY,* flown by Jim Dieffenderfer He remembers;

'*OLD BALDY* released eight 500-lb bombs on a ship from around 6500 ft. Fred Blair, the bombardier, thought they were near enough to stop the ship, but we will never know for at that point AA was heavy

B-17F 41-24381 *PANAMA HATTIE* of the 63rd BS/43rd BG was delivered to the USAAF on 19 June 1942 and sent to the Cheyenne Modification Center one week later, prior to being flown to Australia by Lt Folmer Sogaard and crew. There, it was assigned to the 63rd BS/43rd BG. *PANAMA HATTIE's* nose art was painted by Sgt Ernie Vandal, and it took its name from an old Ann Sothern movie. During the Battle of the Bismarck Sea, on 2 March 1943, Lt Jim Murphy's crew used *PANAMA HATTIE* to sink a freighter, and on the morning of the 3rd Lt William Thompson's crew claimed three fighters shot down with it. In November 1943 *PANAMA HATTIE* was modified by the 4th Air Depot and transferred to the 54th TCG (*via Steve Birdsall*)

Its exterior streaked and stained, B-17F 41-24455 *OLD BALDY* was a multi-mission combat veteran. Sent to the Modification Center at Cheyenne, Wyoming, on 9 July 1942 and then flown to Australia by Lt James G DeWolf, it was assigned to the 63rd BS/43rd BG. *OLD BALDY* returned to the US on 12 November 1943 and was used for training by the 398th BG at Rapid City, South Dakota, and Biggs Field, Texas, before being written off on 3 September 1944 (*www.aerothentic.com*)

The crew of *OLD BALDY* are seen on the wing of B-17F 41-24574 *TUFFY*. They are, from left to right kneeling, Capt James Dieffenderfer (pilot), Lt Jack Campbell (co-pilot), Lt William Grosenburg (navigator) and Lt Fred Blair (bombardier). Standing, from left to right, are T/Sgt Albert Palewicz (engineer/top turret gunner), T/Sgt Rayburn Carroll (radio and waist gunner), S/Sgt James Kersh (aerial engineer and ball turret gunner), S/Sgt Harold Hahn (waist gunner) and S/Sgt Kenneth Mowry (tail gunner) (*Jim Dieffenderfer*)

and I turned towards home. Five to ten minutes after leaving the target Jap fighters jumped us. I went into the clouds, but they were not very thick so we came out and saw fighters dead ahead. I notified the crew as to where they would be coming from. As the crew reported back, the ball turret gunner reported jammed guns. I told him to stay in the turret and keep it moving so the fighters would not know it was not operating. I dived steeply towards the water, where I thought we could defend ourselves better.

'At that time the first fighter made a frontal attack, firing his cannon. As soon as he passed, the control column was jerked out of my hands into full down position. I thought he had shot the controls out. I could not pull the wheel back. I grabbed the co-pilot, Jack Campbell, who was looking out the window trying to follow the fighter, and told him to help me pull the wheel back, or to say a prayer and tell his girlfriend good-bye. We put our feet up on to the

Dressed in their work wear, *OLD BALDY's* groundcrew stand proudly in front of 'their' aircraft in New Guinea on 28 April 1943 (*Jim Dieffenderfer*)

Lt Jim Dieffenderfer is awarded the DFC by Fifth Air Force commander Gen Kenney on 8 June 1943. He received this medal for successfully completing a number of hazardous missions in the first half of 1943 (*Jim Dieffenderfer*)

On 2 March 1943 Lt James Dieffenderfer of the 63rd BS/43rd BG brought *OLD BALDY* back from the Bismarck Sea with its elevators shredded after a 280-mph dive to escape Japanese fighters (*Jim Dieffenderfer*)

B-17F 41-24574 *TUFFY* served in both the 63rd and 403rd BSs whilst with the 43rd BG, flying its last combat mission on 16 October 1943 and returning to the USA 18 days later. Posted to Rapid City, South Dakota, the bomber was also used by the 398th BG as a training aid, before being scrapped at RFC Altus, Oklahoma, sometime after 30 August 1945 (*www.aerothentic.com*)

rudder bar and pulled hard and it came all the way back. I don't remember how many gyrations we went through, but from what the crew said it must have been many. They bent everything they were holding on to. I did not know how much damage had been done to the elevators, so I decided not to move them any more than necessary for they might fall off.

'It crossed my mind to go back and try to assess the damage, but the tail gunner saw the elevators disappear, and was convinced that there was little to see, and hoped I would stay at the controls. I did not know what else might fall off, so we kept the stick still and climbed over the mountains and let down into Port Moresby using the throttles.

'Landing was sure to be a problem. I did not know what might happen to the flight control when speed dropped off. I gave the crew the option of baling out over the field, but they chose to ride it out with me. I decided to make a no-flap landing coming in from the water, so I went out to sea, made a big slow turn back towards the landing strip and passed over the beach at about 500 ft, before starting a slow descent, lowering gear in short applications of toggle switch to make sure I didn't lose control.

'I lucked out and hit the end of the 5000 ft runway, so I lowered full flaps. I couldn't use full brakes. The B-17 had a bad habit of blowing expander tubes and leaving you with no brakes, so I put them on and off and slowed as much as possible before I reached the end of the runway. I unlocked the tail wheel, and as soon I ran into the overrun area I locked the left brake and applied full power to No 4 engine and ground looped the aeroplane, before taxiing to the revetment. Although I missed out on a DFC for my exploits, I did get an "ATT-A-BOY" from Fifth Air Force!'

That same afternoon the B-17s returned to hit the convoy again. Maj Scott in B-17F 41-24574 *TUFFY* dropped two bombs on a large destroyer from 7000 ft and the vessel caught fire. He then dived the B-17, levelling out at 50 ft. His gunners, incensed at the shooting of Moore's crew that morning, blasted away at every survivor in sight.

On the morning of 4 March three 43rd BG B-17s – *Fightin Swede*, *The Mustang* and *Talisman* – found six landing barges near Lae and strafed them until one capsized trying to escape. Two Zeros made repeated attacks on the three Fortresses, slightly wounding the pilot and two crewmen aboard *Fightin Swede*.

B-17F 41-24403 *The Old Man* of the 65th BS/43rd BG is seen at Dobodura following a fight with Zeros over Gasmata on 8 March 1943. *The Old Man* flew its last combat mission on 18 August, after which it was stripped out and converted into a VIP transport for the Fifth Air Force's Gen Enis Whitehead (*US Army via Steve Birdsall*)

B-17F 41-24554 *The* MUSTANG, which flew both with the 19th and 43rd BGs. It completed 109 missions and claimed 17 Japanese aircraft destroyed before being returned to the US as war-weary (*USAF*)

The Battle of the Bismarck Sea ended in defeat for the Japanese. The sinking of nine troop transports and four destroyers was achieved solely by the use of air power.

On 13 March the 43rd BG was again successful in attacks on Japanese shipping when a convoy consisting of a cruiser, two destroyers and five transports, with fighter cover, was spotted. The 63rd BS's Lt Neill Kirby and his crew in *The Reckless Mountain Boys*

dropped flares which enabled Maj Ed Scott in *CAP'N & THE KIDS* to make a successful attack. Kirby then made two runs himself and hit a transport and a destroyer.

On 19 February Kirby had put *The Reckless Mountain Boys* down on the shoreline at Hood Point, south-east of Port Moresby, after running low on fuel returning from a night mission.

On 15 March 64th BS B-17F 41-24424 *Hell From Heaven Men* and most of Lt Arthur McMullan's crew were lost returning from an

B-17F 41-24353 *CAP'N & THE KIDS* flew 80 missions with the 43rd BG before joining the 69th TCS/433rd TCG, 54th TCW. Modified to drop supplies, this Fortress was one of eight war-weary B-17Es that took part in essential operations to deliver weapons, ammunition and medical supplies to Momote Island during the invasion of the Admiralty Islands between 19 February and 4 March 1944. The aircraft participated in further supply drops during the invasion of Hollandia in April 1944 (*Boeing*)

67

abortive mission to Wewak. Out of fuel, McMullan ditched in heavy rain and fog. Only co-pilot Lt Howard G Eberley, bombardier Lt John Dawson and radio operator S/Sgt Robert Freeman managed to get out of the bomber before it sunk. They began swimming, but Freeman could not keep up and he eventually drowned. Eberley and Dawson survived a 14-hour swim to reach safety.

April too was not without its losses. During a night test flight over Port Moresby on the 17th *Dinah Might* and Capt Charles Giddings' crew were involved in a mid-air collision with 41-24425, piloted by Capt Charles N McArthur. Six of McArthur's crew were killed, although Giddings managed to get his crippled Fortress down safely. *Dinah Might* was lost five months later when it was taxied into a ditch on 16 September and had to be written off.

The Reckless Mountain Boys and Capt Byron Heichel's crew in the 63rd BS suffered a fate similar to that of *Hell From Heaven Men* on 7 May. Heichel took off from Seven Mile Strip for a reconnaissance mission with an 11-man crew. Radio operator T/Sgt Clarence S Surrett transmitted back hourly reports on weather and visibility as the B-17 flew on towards Kavieng, the major Japanese naval base on New Ireland. Heichel was forced to turn away when Japanese fighters rose to meet them, and he tried to take cover in cloud, but the fighters soon caught him. They raked the Fortress with machine gun fire, starting a blaze in the port inboard engine and knocking out the ball turret. One of the gunners, S/Sgt Kenneth Vetter, was wounded.

A second fire broke out and the B-17 filled with fumes as Heichel dived for wave-top height. Another fighter attack knocked out the port outboard engine, and Heichel and co-pilot Lt Berry Rucks ditched the crippled bomber about 50 yards off shore. The ball turret caught the coral reef and *The Reckless Mountain Boys* ground to a halt. The top turret was thrown forward, trapping Heichel, but Rucks and the crew freed him. Bombardier Lt Oscar M Linsley, student navigator Lt Eugene Bleiler and waist gunner Sgt Gilbert A Fleiger were killed.

The survivors made it ashore, carrying the badly wounded Vetter and waist gunner S/Sgt James E Etheridge. Natives from Komalu village and labourers from the German-owned Komalu plantation met them. When plantation manager Rudolph Diercke heard about the crash, he sent a note to the survivors and they decided that they had no option but to surrender. All eight were taken to Rabaul and Heichel, Rucks, and Etheridge were eventually transported to a camp in Japan and survived to return to the US.

In May 1943 the 43rd BG began converting to the B-24 Liberator, and in June the 380th BG started flying B-24s from Darwin on long-range missions. In the vast expanse of the Pacific the B-24, with its longer range, was preferred to the B-17, but conversion would not be complete until the end of September.

B-17Fs 41-24520 and 41-24523 were photographed on a test flight from Boeing's Seattle plant in early 1942, prior to being delivered to the 43rd BG. 41-24520 became *Fightin' Swede* in the 63rd BS, where it was named in honour of its pilot, Lt Folmer J Sogaard. Delivered to Lowry on 29 July 1942, this aircraft was based at Hamilton Field, California, from 31 August until being assigned to the 19th BG on 1 September 1942. When the latter group returned to the USA in November of that year, *Fightin' Swede* transferred to the 63rd BS/43rd BG. It was shot down by Japanese fighters whilst being flown by Capt Robert N Keatts' crew somewhere between Finschhafen and Wewak on 8 May 1943. The other Fortress in this photograph, 41-24523, was sent to the Eighth Air Force's 323rd BS/91st BG and was lost in a mid-air collision with B-17F 42-29816 (from the 91st BG's 401st BS) over the English Channel on 31 August 1943. The bomber was participating in its 19th combat mission when lost, and none of its ten-man crew survived (*via Steve Birdsall*)

In the meantime, the 43rd BG continued flying missions in Fortresses. On 6 June B-17E 41-9207 *Texas #6* crashed into the top of Hong Kong Mountain, and amazingly there were four survivors. Local natives led them to a Japanese patrol who executed them on the spot.

On the morning of 16 June, 25-year-old Capt Jay Zeamer Jr, a pilot in the 65th BS, set off on an aerial mapping sortie over the

B-17F 41-24401 *Lakanookie* of the 43rd BG is seen in flight over New Guinea in 1943 (*www.aerothentic.com*)

Solomon Islands. It was his 47th combat mission. The night before, the crew, all volunteers, were told to include a reconnaissance over Buka Passage, as 400 enemy aircraft had just landed there. Zeamer arrived over the target area before the sun had risen high enough to take photos, so he proceeded to Buka first.

With just 45 seconds of the mapping mission remaining, *Lucy,* their B-17E, was attacked by more than 15 fighters. Although mortally wounded, bombardier 2Lt Joseph Sarnoski continued to man his nose-guns and fire at the enemy attackers until he died at his post. Seriously wounded by shrapnel in his legs and both arms, Zeamer manoeuvred *Lucy* for 40 minutes during the combat until the enemy broke off their action, then directed the bomber's flight to a base more than 500 miles away. When Zeamer passed out from loss of blood, top turret gunner Sgt John Able took over, as co-pilot Lt John Britten was also injured. Zeamer, barely conscious, put *Lucy* down at Dobodura, in New Guinea, with one crewman dead and five wounded.

Zeamer hovered on the edge of death for three days, and spent 15 months in more than a dozen hospitals. He and Sarnoski were both awarded the Medal of Honor. With the navigator critically wounded, it was radio operator Bill Vaughan who helped to get them to safety. Although himself severely wounded, he managed to pick up a distant radio signal that gave them an approximate heading to get home. He was awarded the DSC.

Black Jack/The Joker's Wild had at last returned to combat status in April 1943, and it had become something of a lucky ship, being flown by 13 different pilots in the 63rd BS in 14 missions. On 11 July Lt Ralph De Loach flew it when his crew accompanied nine other B-17s on the mission to Vunakanau. The Fortresses were loaded up with 14 wire-strapped 300-lb bombs, 24 20-lb fragmentation bombs and 16 clusters of incendiaries.

They began taking off a little after midnight. Navigation was hampered by bad weather en route, and the Nos 3 and 4 engines on *Black Jack/The Joker's Wild* began malfunctioning. By the time the target was reached one of the

B-17E 41-2481 *Topper* of the 43rd BG crashed on take off from Port Moresby on 27 August 1943 and was written off on 30 October that year. *Topper* had originally been assigned to the 19th BG in Java on 14 February 1942 (*www.aerothentic.com*)

Gen Douglas MacArthur's B-17E (XC-108) 41-2593 *Bataan*, which was one of four B-17E/Fs specially converted into transports under the C-108 designation in 1943. Although an E-model, *Bataan* had a 'blown' B-17F Plexiglas nose with a single 0.50-cal machine gun that boasted a chromed barrel (the only armament carried). The aircraft was also fitted with a navigator's astrodome. A five-man crew and up to 11 passengers could be carried by the XC-108 (*Boeing*)

B-17E 41-2633 *Sally* over Milne Bay on 16 December 1943, with Gen Douglas MacArthur on board. This aircraft had previously served in the 93rd BS/19th BG before being stripped down and furnished with a table, a bunk and a few chairs to become Gen George C Kenney's personal aircraft. It remained as such until two wing spars were cracked in a thunderhead and the veteran bomber had to be retired (*USAF*)

engines had had to be feathered. Bombardier Lt Manuel Diaz got his bombs away, but on the homeward trip it was obvious that *Black Jack/The Joker's Wild* would not make it over the mountain range on New Britain on just three engines. Finally, a severe thunderstorm and the faltering engines made it impossible to hold a straight course and the crew became hopelessly lost.

With fuel running low, De Loach and his co-pilot, Joe Moore, attempted to land on the shallow waters of a reef, but they missed. *Black Jack/The Joker's Wild* was put down in deep water off Bogaboga village in the Milne Bay province of New Guinea – where it was discovered beautifully preserved by three local divers from Lae in 1986.

Three of the crew were injured in the crash, but natives and an Australian coast watcher called Eric Foster rescued all ten men. The next day Foster sent out a radio call, and a small seaplane arrived to take off the wounded and leave supplies for the rest of the survivors. Later, a PT boat arrived to take them to Goodenough Island, where they were flown back to Port Moresby.

B-17s played a small but important role in the successful American paratroop invasion of Nadzab, New Guinea, on 5 September 1943. The top brass wanted to watch the drop, and so 43rd BG CO Col Harry Hawthorne flew *Talisman* with Gen Howard Ramey of V Bomber Command BC in the co-pilot's seat and Gen Douglas MacArthur aboard. Meanwhile, *CAP'N & THE KIDS* was used by Gen George C Kenney, and a third B-17 carried Gen Sutherland. Five modified B-17s followed the C-47s over Nadzab and dropped 300-lb packs throughout most of the day to keep the paratroops supplied.

After Nadzab had been taken, Australian ground troops moved down the Markham Valley towards Lae, and for several days formations of 43rd BG B-17s and B-24s bombed targets in support of the Australian 7th and 9th Divisions. By the end of September 1943 the 43rd BG had converted to the Liberator. Some of the surviving B-17s served as armed transports and troop-carriers, and were still in action as late as May 1944 during the Pacific island-hopping campaign.

THE CACTUS AIR FORCE

In February 1942 the 11th BG at Hickam Field, Hawaii, was training with B-18s when it received B-17s for operations with the newly constituted Seventh Air Force. Col Laverne G 'Blondie' Saunders (so-named because of his coal-black hair) commanded the group when, on 14 June, he took off from Hickam for an audacious moonlight raid on Wake Island. Tail gunner Horst Handrow wrote;

'I flew from Hawaii to Midway Island loaded with bombs and gas and then back for Wake. The moon was bright and everything was perfect for the night raid. Over we roared at 4000 ft with the bomb-bay doors open. We cleaned that place up good. Fires blazed all over the island, and the flak made the night look like the 4th of July.'

Following the raid the 11th BG returned to Hawaii, and soon speculation was rife that they were to proceed to the South Pacific theatre of operations. Late in 1942 the 11th BG left Hawaii and flew via Christmas Island, Canton Island and Fiji to Noumea, capital of New Caledonia, for operations against Guadalcanal where, on 4 July, the Japanese had started building an airfield on the Lunga Plain. Guadalcanal, which is enclosed by the small islands of Tulagi, Gavutu and Tanambogo, is a hilly, tropical, jungle-covered island in the Solomon Islands group. With Lunga airfield complete, the Japanese could send land-based bombers on raids on the New Hebrides for a thrust southwards. As early as April 1942 Tulagi had been deemed the number one US objective in the Solomons, its deep and spacious harbour, with air cover from Guadalcanal, presenting the Japanese with an excellent naval base from which to threaten the lifeline to Australia.

The task of preventing this was given to Vice Adm Robert L Ghormley, Commander South Pacific area (COMSOPAC). His air commander was Rear Adm John S McCain, who controlled all land-based aircraft in the South Pacific area, including those of the USAAF. Maj Gen Millard F Harmon was charged with the training and administration of all US Army ground and air force units in the region.

To avoid overcrowding, Col Saunders left eight 431st BS B-17s at Nandi, on Viti Levu in the Fiji islands, and took the remaining 27 B-17s of the 11th BG to Plaines des Galacs airfield on New Caledonia (the island already accommodated 38 P-39s of the 67th FS and ten B-26s). On arrival at Tontouta, near Noumea, Saunders retained the 42nd BS, but later sent the 98th BS to Koumac, on the north side of the island, and the 26th to Roses Field at Port Vila, on Efate in the New Hebrides. The 11th BG had to be ready for a week of intensive operations against 'Cactus' (the code-name for Guadalcanal) as a prelude to the invasion of the island by US Marines on 7 August 1942.

Rear Adm John S McCain (left), who commanded all land-based aircraft in the South Pacific area, Col (later Brig Gen) Laverne G 'Blondie' Saunders, CO of the 11th BG (centre) and Maj Gen Millard F Harmon, commanding general US Army Forces in the South Pacific area (right)
(*Sam Moses via Bill Cleveland*)

This camouflaged B-17E (41-2426) was assigned to the 43rd BS/11th BG in August 1942. It is seen at the 13th Air Depot at Tontouta, New Guinea, along with a P-38, P-39 and B-26. 41-2426 returned to the US in February 1944 (USAF)

Although an advanced strip was ready on the island of Espiritu Santo, about 150 miles north of Efate, Saunders decided to open his attack from Efate, which possessed better servicing facilities. The 11th BG's ground echelons did not arrive by sea until early September.

The first 900-mile round trip mission to Tulagi Harbour began on schedule on 30 July. The two 431st BS B-17s despatched were badly shot up by Zeros but returned safely with claims of two fighters shot down. The following day two 98th BS B-17s bombed Lunga airfield, Col Saunders flying with Lt Buie's crew. The second B-17E, 41-2616 *The Blue Goose* (so called because it had acquired a light blue gloss paint scheme at the Hawaiian air depot), was flown by Lt Frank 'Fritz' Waskowitz, a former University of Washington football star who had been badly burned in the Pearl Harbor raid. His crew was nicknamed the 'USO kids' because they had once landed at a forward strip and jokingly asked where the nearest USO club was located. Both B-17s achieved almost total surprise, and were only opposed by light flak.

On 1 August the 431st BS moved up from Nandi Field to Efate and then to Espiritu Santo's Button Field. Two days later Horst Handrow, tail gunner in Capt Sullivan's crew, and his fellow crew members were told to get ready for their first crack at Guadalcanal with a raid on the airfield. Handrow wrote;

'After four-and-half hours of flight we saw our target. We were at 12,000 ft. We made our run, and eight 500-lb bombs hit across the runway – two fires were burning very nicely when we left. The anti-aircraft wasn't very heavy because most of the ack-ack batteries had already been put out for keeps. Two Zeros hung over our formation but wouldn't come in to attack – they were radioing our speed and altitude to the ack-ack guns below. We soon left them behind and headed back to our base at Santo.

'More aeroplanes were taking off for 'Canal when we landed. We loaded up again with 20 100-lb bombs, but no orders came through that day so we waited for the next day.

'Rain set in that night. What rotten luck. Death was in the air, because the only landing lights we had were two trucks parked at the end of the runway. We stood there with cold sweat running down our faces. Who wasn't going to make it? We saw an aeroplane light going towards the jungle. "That isn't the runway", I almost shouted. Too late, and with the explosion of gas tanks and the falling of trees the

B-17 went down and started to burn. Five men lost their lives – four got out okay. That was the beginning of our bad luck. We waited out there in the rain with our fingers crossed until they'd all landed.

'We took off again for 'Canal on 4 August, and this time did our bombing at 3000 ft, hitting trucks and supplies – we were so low that you could see the stuff fly up in the air. Seven Zeros were around that day and they would come in once in a while and make a pass at you.'

Eventually the Zeros came in too close and four were shot down. One of the crashing fighters plunged into a 26th BS Fortress flown by Lt R E McDonald and brought that down too – all the crew were lost.

Raids continued on 5 and 6 August and then the Marines landed on 7 August as scheduled. They met no opposition, while the Fortresses conducted unproductive searches at sea for the Japanese fleet to the north of the Solomons. Lt Robert B Loder of the 98th BS was thought to have crashed into the mountains on New Caledonia. Maj Marion N Pharr, the 431st BS CO, also failed to return, and Maj James V Edmundson of the 26th BS assumed command.

On the 8th the Marines reached the newly-built Japanese airfield and discovered that the enemy had fled. The airstrip was renamed Henderson Field after the commander of the Marine dive-bombers at Midway. Meanwhile, the B-17s continued their search at sea. They saw part of the Japanese Navy turning for home with two ships in the task force burning as a result of action in the Solomons area. On 11 August the 11th BG went on a hair-raising low-level photo mission over a Japanese-held island. Horst Handrow remembers;

'We came in at 40 ft with guns going to keep the crews away from the ack-ack batteries. It was real fun. We laid it on the two freighters – we were so close I could see the glass coming down. But the second time through they opened up on us. We put it right back, having all the pictures we wanted, and tailed it for home. Happy day that was.

'Next day we were called out of bed at 0300 hrs and we knew right away that something was up. Our crew jumped into the B-17 and in 15 minutes we were on our way to Guadalcanal, which was being shelled by three Jap cruisers. "Get a cruiser" – those were our orders, and we were out there to fulfil them. All alone, too. As we got in sight of the island we saw a cruiser, but it looked like a light one so we passed it up and started looking for the heavy cruiser which was also in there – we saw it five minutes later while we were flying at 9000 ft.

'We started to circle it, but it slowly circled us so we couldn't make a good run on it. Anti-aircraft fire was coming up, but then with the sun at our backs down we came with bomb-bay doors open until we were at 5000 ft – mighty low to be fooling with anything so big. Out went the bombs – two hits and one close miss, which was not bad for four bombs. She was burning now and all she could do was go around in a

An unidentified B-17E heads towards the coast of Guadalcanal, where a Japanese ship burns off the beach, a victim of an earlier raid (*USAF*)

circle. The cruiser threw everything at us but the boat. We watched for an hour and she was still burning. She sank late that afternoon so the Marines said. It was a job well done, even if we got grounded for three days for getting down that close. I still remembered December 7th.'

On 20 August Henderson Field was repopulated with Wildcats and Dauntlesses. By now the 11th BG had lost 11 B-17s, although only one in combat. Some crews were sent to Fiji for a well earned rest.

Three days later the Navy received warning that the Japanese were moving on the Solomons from the north. Carrier task forces were sent to meet them, and at 1215 hrs on the 24th Col Saunders was advised of a contact with the enemy force some 720 miles from Espiritu. Adm McCain, aware that a B-17 strike would involve hazardous night landings, left the attack decision to Saunders. He accepted the risk, and two flights of Fortresses went off separately.

Three B-17s of the 42nd BS, led by Maj Ernest R Manierre, and four from the 26th BS, led by Maj Allan J Sewart, headed for an area north-west of Santo. Manierre's flight made contact with the task force in the late afternoon and saw the crippled carrier *Ryujo* being towed by a cruiser. On the first run the bombs overshot, and the B-17s went round for another try – this time four direct hits were claimed on the carrier. The *Ryujo* was later sunk by Navy dive and torpedo-bombers.

Sixty miles eastwards, Maj Sewart's four B-17s surprised a second Japanese armada at twilight, and two or more hits were claimed on a large vessel. Zeros then attacked, and five were claimed shot down by the American gunners, with two probables. Two of the B-17s were damaged, and despite all of them being dangerously low on fuel, the flight safely returned to Efate. Manierre's B-17s were not so fortunate – they returned to Santo after dark, and during the landing the Fortress piloted by Lt Robert E Guenther crashed into a hillside after its No 4 engine failed. The pilot and four of the crew were killed.

Missions continued daily from Santo while the airstrip at Henderson Field was made longer for B-17 missions. On 12 September Japanese bombers attacked the base, and the following day enemy ground forces launched heavy attacks. The Marines fought back, and the Japanese were forced to retreat with heavy losses.

B-17s are seen at Guadalcanal's crucially important Henderson Field in January 1943. Built by the Japanese, it was seized by US Marines on 8 August 1942 (*USMC*)

On this occasion *TYPHOON McGOON* of the 98th BS and two B-17s from the 431st BS were lost. Lt Van Haur's *The Spider* and Lt Woodbury's Fortress were forced to ditch, the latter having been hit by flak over New Guinea – one engine was knocked out and the left wing was badly damaged. The B-17 hit the water just after midnight, T/Sgt Ray Storey suffering a badly broken leg in the crash. The crew were picked up the following day, and Van Haur's crew were rescued on 19 September, although by then two men had died from exposure.

By 23 September 1942 the 'Cactus Air Force' was taking positive shape following the arrival at Espiritu Santo of B-17Es of the 72nd BS/ 5th BG, led by Maj Don Ridings. At around this time the units on Santo also began receiving replacement crews and new B-17Fs with more nose-mounted guns. These surprised the Japanese fighter pilots who had been used to making head-on passes against the B-17D/Es.

In mid-October two additional squadrons from the 5th BG arrived, one of which was commanded by Col Brooke E Allen. All three units were placed under the command of 'Blondie' Saunders.

Returning to 23 September, Lt Durbin and the crew of *The Skipper* in the 98th BS dropped incendiaries on the Rekata Bay seaplane base. The B-17 was then attacked by five *Dave* reconnaissance aircraft, but the bomber gunners shot down one and damaged the others.

The following day the 98th BS again tussled with Japanese reconnaissance aircraft. *Galloping Gus,* flown by Capt Walter Y Lucas, and 41-2523 *"GOONIE"*, piloted by Lt Durbin, dropped their 500-lb demolition bombs on cargo vessels in Tonolei Harbour on Fauro Island, off the south-eastern end of Bougainville Island. *The Blue Goose,* flown by Lt 'Fritz' Waskowitz, also dropped bombs successfully, scoring a direct hit on a cargo vessel and near misses on another.

Twenty Nakajima A6M1-N 'Rufe' and E8N1 'Dave' seaplanes had attacked while the 98th BS B-17s made their bombing runs. A 'Rufe' was downed in flames, a 'Dave' was seen to drop away streaming smoke and several other aircraft were hit. Lucas returned to Santo while the damaged *"GOONIE"* and *The Blue Goose* were put down on Henderson Field. None of the crew was injured. The 42nd BS did not fare so well, with Lt Charles F Norton's 41-2420 *Bessie the Jap Basher* ditching in Doma Cove, Guadalcanal, during a search mission.

On 28 September the 11th BG headed for Shortland Island Harbour at the southern end of Bougainville. Horst Handrow wrote;

'I already had a funny feeling when we got into the aeroplane. "Today we are coming back with holes, and lots of them", I said to the mechanics. We got up to Shortland Harbour and it was closed in by a big storm cloud. There were three aeroplanes in our formation. Then out of the clouds the Zeros started coming. I counted 30 in all. Boy, we really were in for it, and I didn't mean maybe – the sky was full of the little sons of a gun, and they started hitting us.

'One went past the tail and I gave him both barrels and down he went in flames. Good shooting, Handrow! Then they started to work my position over. A 20 mm shell hit the tail section and pieces of steel flew all over my position – through the seat I was sitting on, over my shoulder and just buzzing past my leg, burning it more than anything else. "That was close", I thought. Once more they sent bullets through

Maj Rasmussen, CO of the 98th BS/11th BG, stands beside B-17E 41-9214 *The Skipper.* **This aircraft was flown by Lt Durbin on the 23 September 1942 mission to the seaplane base at Rekata Bay, where it tussled with five Japanese B5N 'Kate' torpedo bombers.** *The Skipper's* **gunners were credited with destroying five enemy aircraft during the bomber's first eight missions** (*USAF via Bill Cleveland*)

the door about three feet from me. Then another Zero went out past the tail and I gave him the works – that made two that day. Jim Orr and Pepe got one each too. So four in one day. Not bad shooting.

'After a 20-minute air battle they went home, but not all 30 of them –13 were shot down that day. We'll teach them to fool with our Flying Fortresses! We got a breather when we spotted a Jap cruiser, a nice heavy one. We started our run on it but couldn't get our bombs away so we pulled out of formation to let another ship take our place.'

Waskowitz's *The Blue Goose* pulled in to replace them. On the first run, its bombs failed to release, then on the second run it was attacked by Zeros. Rounds fired into the cockpit of one Zero forced its pilot to rear back, and he pulled the stick with him – this turned his fighter straight up, and it collided with the underbelly of the B-17, which was still loaded with bombs. It exploded in mid-air. Handrow had been in a crew in which Waskowitz was co-pilot. 'Nobody got out. It left me with a cold sweat, and I have feared anti-aircraft fire ever since'.

Fifteen land-based Zeros carrying belly tanks then attacked the returning Fortresses, and in the ensuing battle B-17 gunners claimed eight fighters shot down and two probably destroyed. *"GOONIE"*, flown by Lt Durbin, was hit, and navigator S/Sgt Eber J Nealy was wounded in the head and right thigh when 20 mm cannon and 7.7-in machine gun fire exploded in his compartment. Flak was heavy and accurate, and only two B-17s escaped damage. Handrow concludes;

'We flew back to the 'Canal and landed there on a shot out tyre. Capt White, our pilot, was really on the ball. We looked for more hits and found them all over the aeroplane – 450 in all. The rudder was badly hit, with 17 holes in my little tail section alone. There was also a big hole in the nose and a couple of hits in the No 3 engine. We had a close call, and we were really lucky that nobody got hit. The raid was a flop, but he who runs away today, comes to fight again another day.'

More Japanese and US Marine reinforcements arrived on Guadalcanal in September and October. On 11-12 October the Battle of Cape Esperance was fought at sea off Guadalcanal. On the 12th, Col Saunders, flying with Maj Al Sewart, CO of the 26th BS, led a six-ship formation which took off from Henderson Field for a bombing raid on an airfield just north of the Buka Passage. Maj James Edmundson led the second element with two wingmen from the 431st. He wrote;

'We dropped "thousand-pounders" on the runway. We could see fighters taking off as we were on our bombing run and Zeros were soon at our altitude and continued to work us over as we proceeded south to our second target – a collection of ships at

B-17E 41-9215 *GALLOPING GUS* of the 98th BS/11th BG was photographed at Santo, along with its groundcrew, in 1942. On 24 September Capt Walter Lucas flew this aircraft on a bombing mission to Tonolei Harbour and then returned safely to Santo. This aircraft was finally written off on 15 June 1944 (*Bill Cleveland*)

A veteran of service with both the 98th BS/11th BG and the 5th BG, B-17E 41-2523 *"GOONIE"* was damaged by Japanese fighters on the 24 September 1942 mission to Tonolei Harbour, but its pilot, Lt Walter Lucas, managed to land safely at Henderson Field. *"GOONIE"* was badly damaged again on 29 September – piloted this time by Lt Durbin – returning from a raid on Bougainville when 15 land-based Zeros attacked. Navigator S/Sgt Eber J Nealy was wounded in the head and right thigh by 20 mm cannon and 7.7-in machine gun shells. *"GOONIE"* was credited with seven Japanese aircraft destroyed in only 15 missions, and carried a gold star on its nose denoting its participation in the Battle of Midway. A veteran of 38 days of consecutive combat operations, *"GOONIE"* was eventually lost when its crew (led by 5th BG CO Col M D Unruh) was forced to ditch off the Russell Islands on 30 March 1943. The entire crew was successfully rescued (*USAF via Bill Cleveland*)

anchor in Bum Harbour at the southern end of Bougainville Island. Flak was extremely heavy, and the Zeros stayed with us until we withdrew out of their range. Six Zeros were confirmed as destroyed. All six B-17s received battle damage, several engines were knocked out throughout the formation, several crewmembers were wounded and Ed Lanigan, Al Sewart's navigator, was killed.

'We arrived back over Henderson Field just as a bombardment was under way by about 15 "Bettys" with fighter escort, and the Marine fighters were up after them. We were now low on fuel and out of ammunition, and by the time the field was clear for us to come in and land we were mighty glad to get on the ground.

'That night, 12-13 October, will forever he known as "the night of the big shelling" to all of us who were there. The Japanese had succeeded in getting a task force down "The Slot" (the channel between New Georgia and Santa Isabel Islands north-west of Guadalcanal – author), which included several cruisers and a couple of battleships. They proceeded to lob heavy artillery into Henderson Field throughout the night – several aircraft were hit, and fires were started in the ammunition and fuel dumps. The next morning there was only 2000 ft of usable runway available for those B-17s that were still flyable to take off to return to Espiritu Santo. Lt Hyland, a 42nd BS pilot in *Yokohama Express*, failed to return from a mission on the 12th.'

Meanwhile, the 431st BS had taken off from Button Field for the 'Canal, having changed bomb-loads to 500- and then 1000-lb bombs for a heavy raid on the 13th. Handrow wrote;

'We took off from 'Canal and headed up the string of Solomon Islands to the target – Buka airfield. The weather was bad and we got on the bomb run just as a storm was closing in on the place. Perfect bombing day. We made our run, four "thousand pounders" going right down the middle of the runway. The other formation dropped 60 "hundred pounders" on the parked aeroplanes. A nice couple of fires were started, and 14 aeroplanes won't be flying any more.

'Anti-aircraft fire was coming up, but it wasn't too good. Three Zeros started attacking us, and hit two ships in our formation. Then they went after us, but we did okay. I got one as he went past the tail – he went down like a spinning wheel on the 4th of July! The other ship's gunner got one. He just blew up above us and the pieces went right past the tail. It looked pretty good. Again we had some more holes. I got two more through my section. Back to Guadalcanal we went, and were grounded because of no oxygen system.

'On 12 October we took off for Santo. "Peaceful Santo" we called it. That night was hell on Guadalcanal because the Japs came in with half their fleet and shelled the place all night. Five Fortresses were caught on the ground. The gas works went up too, and there were only 85 gallons of gas left for 85 aeroplanes – not enough to send up even a couple of dive-bombers.

'On 15 October we took off from Santo to bomb the Jap fleet shelling the 'Canal. Our orders were to get the two transports unloading men and guns. We'd rather have gone after some bigger bait, but orders are orders. Twelve aeroplanes were in the formation. We went in in waves of threes, and we were in the second wave. I have never seen the ack-ack so thick. Down went our bombs, and four "500-pounders" hit – blew it all to heck. What a sight! The water was full of swimming Japs. The third wave hit a battleship and left it burning.

'Then seven Zeros attacked out of the sun. One went past, but I couldn't get in a very good shot. Then one started in on my tail. Was this guy nuts? They never do it because it's sure death, yet here he was coming, and getting closer. I started firing with all I had, but he kept on coming. Was he going to ram us? I kept on firing – 200 rounds had already gone his way. Boy, I was sweating blood. He was only 25 yards away, and I would have got out of the tail. He was out to get us, and he almost did – what a life I led! Back to Santo we went, me with more holes in the tail!'

B-17E 41-2525 *MADAME-X* of the 98th BS/11th BG undergoes repairs in the Solomons in 1942. This aircraft, which was named after a pre-war movie and flown by Lt Cope, eventually transferred to the 31st BS/5th BG and was written off at Kahili on 6 June 1943 (*USAF via Bill Cleveland*)

Zeros were not the only Japanese air menace in the Solomons. On 16 October the 72nd BS crew led by Lt Thompson tussled with a Japanese four-engined flying boat while on a routine search mission east of Santa Isabel Island, about 60 miles from Rekata Bay. The battle lasted 20 minutes, at the end of which the flying boat was shot down after making a futile attempt at trying to escape into some scattered cloud. Sgt White, the engineer and ball turret operator, was hit in the eye by shattered glass when a 20 mm shell hit the turret.

The following day a flight of six B-17s took off from Santo at around 1430 hrs to bomb Japanese supplies and installations in the vicinity of the Kokumbona River – they arrived at the target shortly before dark, and bombed in two elements on the target area. Some 12 tons of demolition bombs were laid squarely on an ammunition dump, and crews felt the concussion at 10,000 ft. They returned to Santo at 2230 hrs in the middle of a heavy rainstorm. Despite this, all the B-17s landed safely, although most had to make as many as three attempts.

On 18 October the 42nd BS moved up from Plaines des Oalacs to Turtle Bay on the south-east corner of Santo, where the B-17s would be nearer their targets. By using Henderson Field as a staging post, they could save on precious fuel, sent in by drums and poured into the bombers' tanks from buckets and cans. Fuel was always scarce.

So Sully Please, flown by Lt Williams, was packed 'from bombsight to tail' with an assortment of provisions, mess components and cooks, medical personnel and luggage so that a mess could be established on Santo. But crews were soon to discover that Turtle Bay was no paradise on earth – rain fell daily, and dengue fever and malaria were prevalent. Santo was also under constant threat from seaborne and aerial attack. The 98th BS's base was bombed four times, and twice during October it was shelled by submarines. However, the only damage was when an 800-lb bomb felled a tree, which in turn crushed the wing of a B-17.

B-17E 41-9122 *Eager Beavers* of the 72nd BS/11th BG taxies in on two outboard engines at Henderson Field in an effort to save precious fuel, which was always in short supply in the Solomons. This Fortress later transferred to the Thirteenth Air Force (*USAF*)

B-17F 41-24457 *The AZTEC'S CURSE* of the 26th BS/11th BG is flown by Capt Walter Chambers over the Rendova Islands, in the Solomons, after bombing Gizo Island on 5 October 1942. Subsequently passed on to the 31st BS/5th BG, this aircraft was written off on 30 April 1945 (*via Bill Cleveland*)

Santo soon became overcrowded, with the 98th BS/11th BG, being joined by the 5th BG, led by Col Brooke E Allen, and some New Zealand air and ground units. Even so, although taking off in formation from the one-way strips at the crowded bases was difficult, operations continued unabated against enemy positions on Guadalcanal, and the neighbouring islands of Tulagi, Gavutu and Tanambogo.

The 5th BG, flying both B-17s and B-24s, had left Hickam Field in November 1942. It joined the Allied drive from the Solomons to the Philippines, flying long patrol and photographic missions over the Solomons and the Coral Sea, attacking shipping off Guadalcanal, and raiding airfields in the northern Solomons until August 1943.

November proved to be the decisive month in the six-month Guadalcanal campaign. The Japanese made several large-scale attempts to land forces on the island and drive the Marines into the sea – US naval forces were hard-pressed, and most of the enemy fleet units that were stopped fell prey to small numbers of ships and aircraft.

By this time the squadrons of the 11th BG were operating regularly from Henderson Field. Japanese air raids happened daily, and Imperial naval forces shelled the field frequently. There was also 'Pistol Pete', the name given to several Japanese gun positions in the hills surrounding the field. These made life unpleasant for the air and groundcrews.

Nevertheless, the B-17s made life really unpleasant for the Japanese. On 13 November, following a reconnaissance mission during which the Japanese battleship *Hiei* was spotted, two Fortresses from the 19th BG were sent to try to bomb it. Sgt Frank Hohmann, engineer in Capt Rousek's crew in B-17E 41-9209 *Blues in the Nite*, recalls;

'The mission was our first with the skip-bombing technique. It was a night flight taking off from Port Moresby 24 minutes after midnight. The other B-17 developed engine trouble and returned to base. Our route took us south of Rabaul out to Bougainville, where we turned south well out from the coast, west of Empress Augusta Bay, and flew south-east for the Buin/Faisi area on Shortland Island. We had the sun coming up in our eyes at a perfect position.

'We closed in on Shortland and flew down low over the land and coastline, topped a low ridge of a point of land, dropped down to 200 ft and couldn't miss the battleship just sitting there all alone and all dark. They had no idea what hit them. Alton D Leaman, our tail gunner, reported where our bombs landed, and there was only small arms fire, but in the wrong direction from our path. One bomb landed in the water close to the starboard side about two-thirds from the bow. The second landed just inside the starboard rail. The third landed about three-quarters the width of the ship and the last bomb landed on the port side and glanced off the deck into the water. The whole crew got a second Air Medal for this one mission.'

The 11th BG sent 17 B-17s to finish off the damaged battleship, which was limping along north-west of Savo. One direct hit and five probables were scored, and the ship finally sank several days later.

During a routine search the following day, Capt Joham and his crew in *TYPHOON McGOON II* from the 98th BS spotted a large task force, including two carriers, north-west of Guadalcanal. Joham's radio operator notified Naval Command, while *TYPHOON McGOON II* maintained a vigil high above the fleet. The ships opened up. Six Zeros and one 'Rufe' were soon joined by others, and they attacked the B-17 through the flak. Six fighters were claimed destroyed by the Fortress gunners before the aircraft limped home at 1600 hrs, riddled with cannon and machine gun fire. Projectiles had ripped the tail of the B-17 almost to shreds, yet the tail gunner had survived unharmed.

Thanks to Capt Joham and his crew, the 11th BG, naval surface vessels and aircraft and the Marine Air Group at Guadalcanal were able to find and attack the task force near Savo Island. The Fortresses, together with SBD Dauntlesses and TBF Avengers from Henderson Field, sank or severely damaged eight of the vessels. Next morning searches revealed many Japanese ships burning and sinking over a wide expanse of sea around Savo Island. Capt Lucas in *Buzz King* led four other 98th BS B-17s to score direct hits and effective near misses on troop transports, and two US battleships finished off the task force, sinking one battleship, two cruisers and several smaller ships.

On 18 November, Col 'Blondie' Saunders, in 26th BS B-17 41-24531, piloted by Maj Sewart and Lt Jack Lee, led ten B-17s, each loaded with cargoes of 1000-lb armour-piercing bombs, up the 'Slot' against Japanese shipping at Tonolei Harbour on Buin. Capt Darby's 72nd BS B-17 got stuck in a shell hole at Henderson Field but took off later. Darby's crew would account for a Zero destroyed.

Capt Lucas in *Buzz King*, Lt Durbin in *Omar Khayyam, The Plastered Bastard* and Lt Morgan in *Galloping Gus* (all 98th BS pilots) scored direct hits on a cargo vessel and several misses. A 20 mm shell shattered the glass and damaged the interior of the ball turret in Morgan's B-17, but no injuries

B-17E 41-9211 *TYPHOON McGOON II* (the first was lost on 13 September 1942) of the 98th BS/11th BG sits amongst the palm trees on New Caledonia in January 1943. Capt Joham's crew was flying this aircraft when they spotted a large Japanese task force north-west of Guadalcanal on 14 November 1942. Note the MV (air-to-surface-vessel) 'whisker brooms' search radar antennae protruding from the upper nose (two more of which were fixed under the wings) and six Japanese kills – all claimed shot down on the 14 November mission (*USAF via Bill Cleveland*)

were reported. Maj Whitaker and Lt Thomas Classen, both 72nd BS pilots, were attacked by Zeros, probably based at Buin airfield. Classen's crew claimed two fighters destroyed.

After the bombing run, 20 Zeros made head-on attacks on the formation. A burst raked Saunders' command ship, nicking Maj Sewart's arm and hitting Lt Lee in the ankle. Saunders went back to get a first-aid kit, and returned to the flight deck just as a Zero fired a second burst into the cabin, sending a 7.7-in round through Sewart's heart, killing him instantly. Lee was hit in the stomach. He fell back, and Saunders lifted him from the co-pilot's seat so that he could take the controls of the badly damaged B-17, which was flying with an engine out and another damaged. The left wing was blazing from escaping fuel from the wing tank, and the only instrument still working was the clock! Saunders told another B-17 to take the lead. He later wrote;

'From the co-pilot's seat I couldn't trim the tabs and handle the aeroplane with those two dead engines on the left, so I got the pilot's body out and moved into the pilot's seat. I decided to make for some overcast and so we dived down. The left wing was red hot. The bank and turn indicator showed we were in a spin. We came out of the overcast at about 500 ft and I saw I'd have to put her down. This was about 20 minutes after the pilot and co-pilot had been hit. Other aeroplanes stayed around to protect us but the Zeros didn't follow us that far. I told the other aeroplanes to take our position, and then headed for a little island in order to come down as close to land as possible.'

Saunders successfully ditched the faltering bomber just offshore at Vella Lavella, on Ballale Island, although he cut his head when he banged into the windshield putting the B-17 down on the water at 95 mph – the wings hit and the bomber came to an abrupt stop. Saunders and navigator Lt Donald G O'Brien slid through the cockpit window, whilst the rest of the crew got out through a break in the fuselage after the tail broke off. Bombardier Lt Nelson Levi, who had been badly wounded in the thigh, and Lt Lee were carefully extricated from the bomber and placed in two liferafts. Lee died as they paddled ashore.

Natives found the airmen and took them to a village. From his camouflaged tree-top lookout, Australian coastwatcher Jack Keenan had seen the B-17 crash. He made contact with the survivors and notified Guadalcanal by radio. The following afternoon a PBY Catalina, escorted by three Wildcats, picked up the men and returned them to Santo.

November had seen the beginning of the end of Japanese attempts to retake Guadalcanal, and they withdrew to the islands in the north. Three sea battles took place off Guadalcanal, culminating in the Battle of Tassafaronga on 30 November. The B-17s were put on stand-by.

Although many of the decisive battles for the control of Guadalcanal took place at sea, the 11th and 5th BGs flew support missions throughout, bombing Japanese ground forces and shipping. One of their frequent missions was against the 'Tokyo Express', the Japanese combat and transport ship task force that plied the 'Slot' almost nightly to reinforce hard-pressed ground troops on the embattled island.

Meanwhile, the Japanese built a new airfield in a coconut grove at Munda on the New Georgia islands, leaving the coconut trees standing until the last minute, then felling them and filling in the holes so that

B-17E 41-2531 *Buzz King* of the 98th BS/11th BG on Santo in 1942. During the Christmas Eve 1942 strike against enemy shipping off Rabaul, heavy fuel consumption forced the aircraft's pilot, Capt Durbin, to return to Guadalcanal early. The aircraft had the best record of any B-17 in the group, with ten Japanese aircraft claimed shot down and three hits on surface ships (*USAF via Bill Cleveland*)

B-17E 41-2659 *Frank Buck* of the 28th BS/19th BG, which later transferred to the 43rd BG at Port Moresby and was written off on 31 October 1944. The nickname came from the wild animal trapper who always promised to 'bring 'em back alive'. Truly a combat weary by 1943, having first arrived in-theatre in March 1942, 41-2659 was reckoned by most crews to be the 'worst ship' in the squadron! (*B T Stout via Steve Birdsall*)

the field was ready for Zeros the next day. Horst Handrow recalls;

'We got word that Japs were out again, so every aeroplane was on double alert on 1 December. Capt Willis 'Jake' Jacobs of the 431st BS (flying B-17F 41-24534 *Omar Khayyam, The Plastered Bastard*) got shot down on a search mission over New Georgia, Vella Lavella. A Zero rammed them, and only one man (Cpl Joseph Hartman, the tail gunner) got out. Hamalainen, my old radioman, went down in that ship.'

Hartman was rescued later, and he confirmed that the crew had shot down three enemy fighters.

On 10 December the first escorts ever used in the area accompanied the B-17s to Munda Point. The twin-engined P-38 Lightnings were a welcome addition, since as many as 40 Japanese fighters rose to meet the bomber formations. The fighters shot down five attacking Zeros while B-17s gunners claimed two more. Some of the Zeros flew between 1500-4000 ft above the B-17s and dropped bombs with timed fuses – crews reported some 20 bursts from these bombs.

Maj Whitaker, 72nd BS CO, returned alone to Guadalcanal and was attacked by Zeros. Four 20 mm shells hit one wing and one exploded in the other. Whitaker landed safely, but the main spar was damaged to such an extent that the B-17 had to be sent to the depot for major repairs. Another bomber, piloted by Maj Gloher and Capt Carl Coleman, on a search in the Bougainville sector, returned with an engine out and another damaged. Coleman lay dead in his seat, killed by a 7.7-in bullet, which had entered the cabin below the windshield.

For three days running – 19-21 December – the B-17s attacked Munda again. Larger craters littered the airstrip and prevented the Zeros from taking off. Meanwhile, pressure was applied to Kahili airfield on Bougainville's south-east tip. On the morning of the raid on the 19th, Capt Charters and his crew in the 98th loaded their B-17E *The Skipper* with 100-lb bombs, several 20-lb fragmentation bombs and two baskets of 'secret weapons' – actually beer bottles! For two hours in the dark early morning, *The Skipper* remained over Kahili, dropping bombs every 15 minutes. Japanese searchlights probed the skies during the first bomb runs, but were suddenly and completely extinguished when the crew hurled out two of their 'secret weapons'!

On Christmas Eve 1942 the 11th BG took off from Guadalcanal between 2100 and 2300 hrs for a strike against enemy shipping concentrating at Rabaul. Capt Durbin of the 98th BS, in *Buzz King*, was forced to return early after heavy fuel consumption, and a B-17 in the 431st BS also had to turn back early. Horst Handrow recalls;

'We took off in '59 (B-17E 41-2659 *Frank Buck/Bring 'Em Back Alive*), the worst ship in the 98th BS – we had 20 minutes' gas to spare if we made it up and back! It was a sweat mission. Fifteen minutes out of Rabaul No 4 engine went out, so we turned around and started back.

Thirty minutes later No 2 engine went out and that left two. We dropped our bombs in the Pacific to lighten the load, then No 1 started to act up and it looked like we were going to sit the B-17 down in the Pacific with Japs all around us. But luck was with us and we made it okay – we came in with ten minutes' gas left. It was '59's last flight.

'The other B-17s dropped their 500-lb armour-piercing bombs on 50 ships in Rabaul Harbour. Maj Lucas in *TYPHOON McGOON* and Capt Crane in 41-2523 *"GOONIE"* – both 98th BS pilots – made runs together, scoring three direct hits on a large troop transport and damaging two others. The strike force returned to base and killed the tail gunner of a Japanese four-engined flying boat who was demonstrating a machine gun the emperor had given him for Christmas.'

"GOONIE" was later ditched off the Russell Islands on 20 March 1943. Col Marion D Unruh, 5th BG CO, and his crew were rescued.

On 28 December Lt James Harp and his crew in the 42nd BS were lost when their B-17 was shot down. Capt Donald M Hyland was also shot down, but he and his crew were rescued later by a US Navy PBY.

Two days later Col Saunders handed over command of the 11th BG to Col Frank F Everest. 'Blondie' was well respected by his men, and he had led them through many battles. He was promoted to brigadier general and was later chief of staff, B-29 operations, commanding the 58th BW before he had to retire after losing a leg in a flying accident.

On 4 January 1943 the Japanese Imperial staff finally issued orders for the evacuation of Guadalcanal to begin. On the 13th the 5th and 11th BGs came under the control of XIII Bomber Command (Col Harlan T McCormick), Thirteenth Air Force (Maj Gen Nathan F Twining), established on Espiritu Santo. January 1943 was occupied mainly by search missions, with a few bombing strikes on Bougainville and the Russell Islands, north of Guadalcanal. On 1 February the depleted 42nd BS/11th BG, which was now down to just four B-17s, suffered a severe blow when three crews failed to return from a shipping strike in the Shortland-Bougainville area. Capt Houx's B-17 was hit in the bomb-bay by flak and disintegrated in the air. Shortly afterwards 41-2442 *Yokohama Express*, flown by Capt Harold P Hensley, and the other B-17E, flown by Capt Hall, were downed by Zeros.

By 9 February the last remnants of the Imperial Army had been evacuated from 'Canal by sea. Two days earlier, the official order relieving the 11th BG from duty was signed. In March 1943 the group returned to the Hawaiian Islands and was reassigned to the Seventh Air Force. From May to November the 11th re-equipped with B-24 Liberators and then returned to the Pacific.

The 5th BG, now led by Col Unruh, moved to Henderson Field on 20 August. A short time before, Lt Alfred Cohen, a 21-year-old replacement navigator, had joined the 23rd BS. He recalls;

'The group had lost a lot of navigators in Japanese frontal attacks, and to malaria. I was one of 15 volunteers who had put in for immediate duty, thinking that I would be posted to North Africa. I had always wanted to see Cairo. Imagine the shock when I opened my orders aboard a packed converted Liberator transport to learn that I was headed for APO 709-SOPAX-South Pacific, Guadalcanal! I went cold and started to shake.

B-17E 41-2428 *OLE SH'ASTA* of the 98th BS/11th BG at Santo in 1943. Note the Midway star. This Fortress was lost in January 1943 (*USAF via Bill Cleveland*)

'On arrival at Espiritu Santo I was assigned to the crew of Capt Tex Burns, soon to be the 23rd BS CO, whose navigator had been killed. The group had B-17E/Fs, mostly battered Es, some of which were from Hickam at the time of the attack on Pearl Harbor! Burns, 26, tall and lean, and a wonderful pilot, asked if I had any gunnery training. I said I hadn't. "Well", he said, "we're off to Guadalcanal tomorrow".

'I flew my first mission, to an airbase east of Bougainville, that first night. We had our briefing sitting on the ground – when I got there the crew were sitting around the place, and it was more like a Boy Scout jamboree. Burns asked me the time – my throat was already constricted with fear. I was 21 and scared, and shrilled the reply. Burns, I was to discover, was brave and democratic, a great gambler from Texas University where he had graduated as an engineer. The ops officer decided bomb-bay loads, and said we must hit *something* that night: "Go up and hit targets of opportunity" he said. The 5th BG had flown night missions and had run into nightfighters, so they had then gone in during the day. A lot of missions were designed to hit targets at dawn, leaving at 0300 hrs. It was more like World War 1, really.

'To accompany me I had my tent-mate Sid Ingrams, a bombardier from North Carolina (they always sent someone along to accompany a new recruit on his first mission). We got off on the mission and over the target. As we approached, Ingrams said, "It's just a milk-run – if you think this is bad, you should have been here when it was rough!" Then we were caught in some lights. Fireworks! Up came tracer. It looked like strings of pearls. I looked for Ingrams. He was crouched under the navigator's table! We dropped our bombs and came home.

'Flying in the Pacific was totally different to Europe. We flew in shirtsleeves. We didn't wear 'chutes. One day we found out they were rotten – when you took your shoes off for bed the next morning they would be green with mould. On searches we flew at under 1000 ft, sometimes lower – even 100 ft. These searches were over ten hours, and all of them over water. It was easy to get lost. If we were bombing land targets, sometimes we flew at 20,000 ft, sometimes 3000 ft – it was never the same.

'We flew formations that were mixed. As navigator, I often stood behind the pilots when I was not actually navigating, and as the Liberators opened their bomb-bay doors, I could see under them. B-17 pilots struggled to keep from sliding under the B-24s. Throttles were always all the way back and the warning horns – the landing gear warning – in our B-17s were always going non-stop! We didn't do squadron bombing or navigating. The B-17 was claustrophobic.

'The most frightening thing I ever saw was a Jap nightfighter over Kahili shooting down our B-17 wingman before we made our bomb run. I saw his exhaust and then the double lines of orange-red tracer – and suddenly that B-17 was a ball of fire and just dropped out of the sky. It was probably a Zero that was responsible. I said to pilot Dean Lucas, a Mormon from Salt Lake City, "Did you see that?" He said, "Yes – we go in". The gunner said, "Do we have to?"

'There was no glamour in the Pacific, but at Christmas 1943, when our ten remaining B-17s were flown back to the US, it was beautiful – mist and sun off their wings as they flew away.'

The 5th BG crew of *LIL NELL* at Henderson Field on 15 August 1943. They are, from left to right, back row, S/Sgt Hildebrand (engineer), Capt A D Lucas (pilot), Lt W L Chestnut (co-pilot), Lt Alfred B Cohen (navigator) and Lt W A Hodges (bombardier). Front row, from left to right, Cpl Waselowski (assistant engineer), Cpl Granowski (assistant radio man), Sgt Hamaker (tail gunner) and Sgt Fredricks (radio operator, killed in action in September 1943). Following their final use in Alaska on the 13 February 1943 mission to Kiska Harbour, all B-17s in this theatre were redeployed to the South Pacific. By mid-1943, most Fortresses had been withdrawn from the Pacific in favour of the longer-range B-24 Liberator, which was better suited for operations there, having a higher speed and bigger bomb-load at medium altitudes. The censor has obliterated the fuselage aerial in this photograph (*Alfred B Cohen*)

APPENDICES

B-17 GROUP ASSIGNMENTS, PACIFIC THEATRE 1942-43

7th BG
Air echelon Java 14 January-1 March 1942

V Bomber Command
(South-West Pacific)

XIII Bomber Command
(South Pacific)

Fifth Air Force
19th BG
28th*, 30th, 93rd and 435th BSs
23/10/41 Clark Field, Luzon
24/12/41 Batchelor, Australia
30/12/41 Singosari, Java
18/4/42 Garbutt Field, Australia
18/5/42 Longreach, Australia
24/7-23/10/42 Mareeba, Australia
Returned to US 1/11/42
* on 22 February 1942 the 28th BS became
the 435th BS within the 19th BG

Thirteenth Air Force
11th BG
26th, 42nd, 98th and 431st BSs
July 1942 New Hebrides
8/4/43 Hickam Field, Hawaii
to Seventh Air Force March 1943 and trained with B-24s

5th BG
23rd, 31st, 72nd and 394th BSs
1/12/42 Espiritu Santo
19/8/43 Guadalcanal
Converted to B-24s December 1943

43rd BG
63rd, 64th, 65th and 403rd BSs
28/3/42 Sydney, Australia
1/8/42 Torrens Creek, Australia
14/9/42 Port Moresby, New Guinea
10/12/43 Dobodura, New Guinea
Converted to B-24s May-September 1943

All drawings on the following three pages
are of a Boeing B-17E Flying Fortress at
1/108th scale. Increase in size by 1.5 to
achieve 1/72nd scale

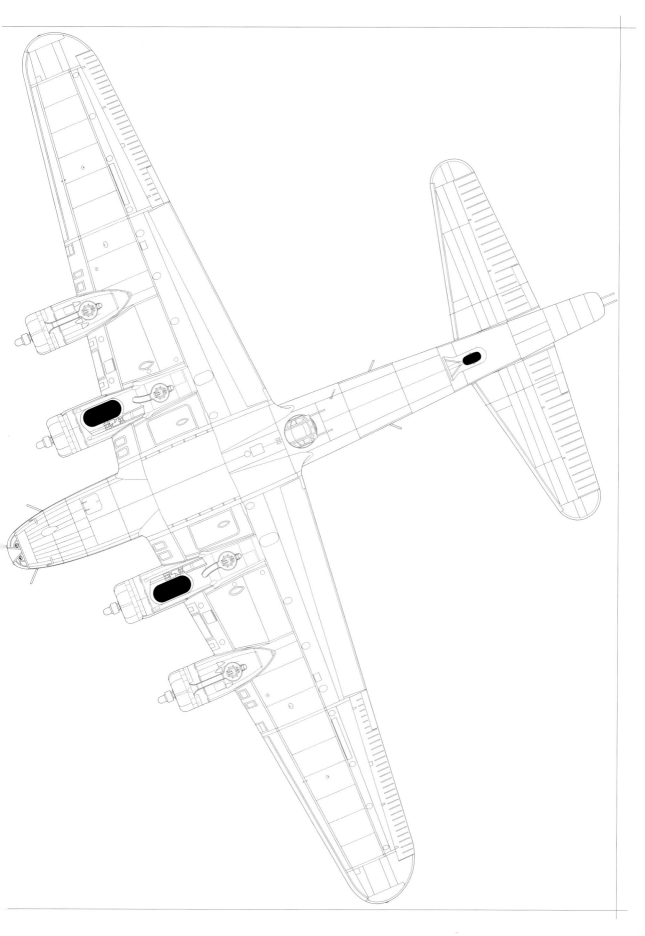

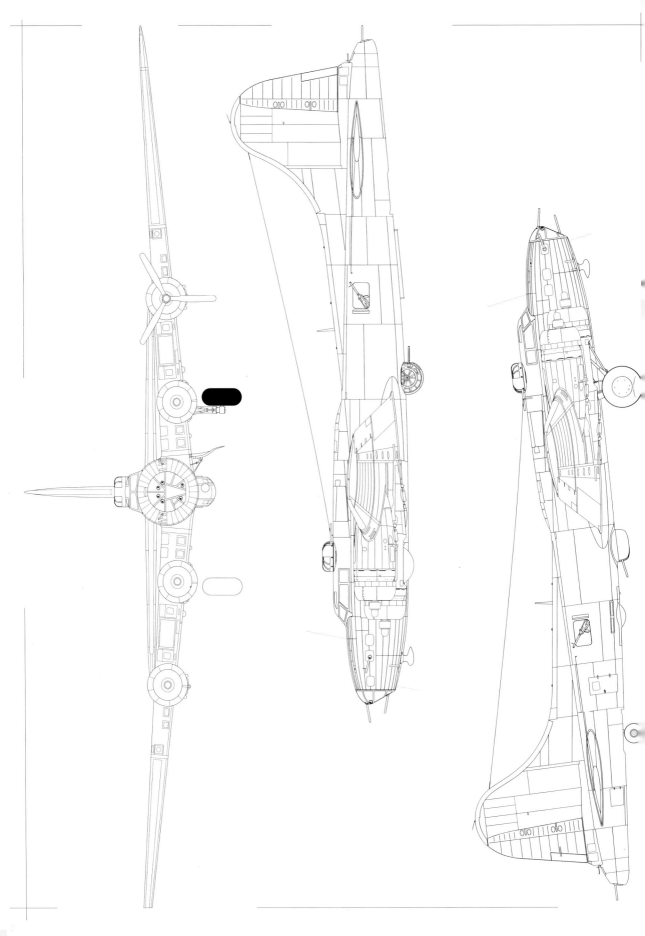

COLOUR PLATES

1
B-17D 40-3097 *"THE SWOOSE"* of the 19th BG, South-West Pacific, 1942-43

This famous aircraft, whose name originated from the song of the time which referred to Alexander, half swan, half goose, is the oldest known surviving B-17, and the only D-model in existence. Assigned to the 19th BG at Hickam Field, Hawaii, on 14 May 1941, *"THE SWOOSE"* fought in Java from 30 December 1941 before being used as a personal hack for Lt Gen George M Brett, CO Allied Air Forces in Australia, flying an estimated 4000 hours as his command transport, and later as a VIP transport. It set several speed records, including a 5 hr 10 min crossing from Sydney, Australia, to Woodbourne, New Zealand, on 17 November 1944. The aircraft returned to the US later that same month, where it made at least three cross-country war-bond tours. Flights to Central and South America followed, before it was sent to the War Assets Aviation Surplus Base at Kingman, Arizona. Col Frank Kurtz, who piloted *"THE SWOOSE"* during the war, led a successful rescue bid to save the bomber from the smelter's torch and have the B-17D brought back to Los Angeles as a war memorial. The city of Los Angeles failed to provide a display home for the bomber, however, and in January 1949 the *"THE SWOOSE"* was flown to Illinois for storage, pending further plans. Finally, it was given to the National Air Museum (now the National Air and Space Museum) in Washington DC, and after being displayed outside for several years it was dismantled and stored in Building 23 at the Paul E Garber facility at Silver Hill, Maryland, where it presently awaits full restoration.

2
B-17E 41-2417 *MONKEY BIZZ-NESS* of the 63rd BS/43rd BG, South-West Pacific, 1942

Delivered to the Salt Lake City Service Air Depot (SAD) on 19 January 1941 and assigned to the 19th BG in Hawaii, this aircraft was transferred to Java on 19 February 1942. It crashed in Queensland, Australia, on 6 July 1942 when it was being piloted by Lt William Thompson, and was salvaged.

3
B-17E 41-2428 *"OLE" "SH'ASTA"* of the 98th BS/11th BG, South Pacific, 1942-43

Delivered to Salt Lake SAD on 26 November 1941 and assigned to the 98th BS/11th BG at Hickam Field on 26 October 1942, this aircraft was lost in January 1943.

4
B-17E 41-2430 *naughty but nice* of the 43rd BG, South-West Pacific, 1942-43

Delivered to Salt Lake City SAD on 30 November 1941, this aircraft was assigned to the 88th RS/7th BG at Hickam Field and arrived in Hawaii in the midst of the Japanese attack on Pearl Harbor on 7 December 1941. The B-17 survived the bombing and was transferred to the 19th BG, before being re-allocated for a third time to the 43rd BG. 41-2430 was shot down on the mission to Vunakanau on 26 June 1943, and only navigator Lt Holguin survived as a PoW.

5
B-17E 41-2432 *The LAST STRAW* of the 63rd BS/43rd BG, South-West Pacific, 1942-43

Delivered to Salt Lake City SAD on 30 November 1941 and assigned to the 88th RS/7th BG, this aircraft also landed at Hickam Field during the Japanese attack on Pearl Harbor. Having also survived the bombing, it was transferred to the 40th RS, and then the 28th BS/7th BG, before being re-allocated to the 19th BG. *The LAST STRAW* finished combat in early September 1943 and went to the 443rd TCG on 8 December, being written off on 12 January 1945.

6
B-17E 41-2440 *Calamity JANE* of the 98th BS/11th BG, South Pacific, 1942-43

Delivered to Salt Lake City SAD on 21 November 1941 and assigned to the 40th RS/19th BG at Hickam Field on 26 December 1941, this aircraft subsequently transferred to the 11th BG. It eventually returned to the US on 7 March 1944, being stored at Lambert, Montana, and Chanute Field until 1 February 1945. The bomber was duly reclaimed on 15 July 1946.

7
B-17E 41-2458 *YANKEE DIDD'LER* of the 65th BS/43rd BG, South-West Pacific, 1942-43

Delivered to Sacramento on 17 December 1941 and assigned to the 28th BS/19th BG, this aircraft flew to Java on 30 January 1942 and later transferred to the 65th BS/43rd BG. Veteran Reginald Tatro recalls;

'I flew to Sydney aboard the *YANKEE DIDD'LER* on a beer run to purchase liquor for the Enlisted Men's Club. Upon landing, the Aussie women tower controllers were shocked at the nose art, so they made us park out of sight – in other words from the public. It also said, "Wouldn't It Root Ya?" The guys of the early era of the 65th didn't realise the Aussie interpretation of the word "root"!'

YANKEE DIDD'LER was sent to the 317th TCG at Dobodura in November 1943 and was written off on 27 January 1945.

8
B-17E 41-2463 *YANKEE DOODLE* of the 19th BG, South-West Pacific, 1942-43

Delivered to Geiger Field on 28 December 1941 and assigned to the 19th BG at Hickam Field on

13 February 1942, *YANKEE DOODLE* was written off on 13 August 1943.

9

B-17E 41-2472 GUINEA PIG of the 7th BG/19th BG, Java and South-West Pacific, 1942

Delivered to McChord Field, Washington, on Christmas Eve 1941 and assigned to the 7th BG in Java on 15 January 1942, the bomber later transferred to the 19th BG in Australia and finally to the 43rd BG. During its long career *GUINEA PIG* flew more than 200 missions before finally being written off on 31 August 1944.

10

B-17E 41-2483 MORMON METEOR of the 7th BG/19th BG, Java, February 1942

Delivered to Sacramento on 28 December 1941 and assigned to the 19th BG in Java on 31 January 1942, *MORMON METEOR* was blown up at Madioén on 28 February when the airfield was evacuated, thus preventing the unserviceable aircraft from falling into enemy hands.

11

B-17E 41-2489 SUZY-Q of the 93rd BS/19th BG, Mareeba, Australia, September 1942

One of the most famous Fortresses of the Pacific War, 41-2489 was delivered to MacDill on 4 January 1942 and assigned to the 93rd BS/19th BG on 7 February 1942. The bomber took part in all the Pacific battles except Midway, and its gunners claimed no less than 26 Japanese aircraft shot down. *SUZY-Q* was named after the wife of its first pilot. Maj Felix Hardison, CO of the 93rd BS. His bombardier, Durwood Fesmire, wrote;

'*SUZY-Q* was a lucky ship and no one was ever killed or wounded in her, although that goes for all the ships I flew while in the SWPA. We didn't ever get into any real trouble with fighters. The best defence was to try and fly at 30,000 ft, as the Zero got really sloppy on the controls at that height and couldn't stay with you. They usually attacked singly, and in the early days attacks were all from the tail. When we got the E-model they started coming in from the front, When the 19th BG was gradually withdrawn, most of the old timers were sent back to the States. They flew *SUZY-Q* home too for a flag-waving tour. She was a great ship, but then what B-17 wasn't?'

When the 19th BG retreated to Mareeba in September 1942, *SUZY-Q* was one of the proud remnants. The bomber eventually returned to the US, arriving at Hamilton Field, California, on 23 October 1942. After being shuttled through a variety of training bases, it finished its days at San Bernardino and was scrapped in mid-1946.

12

B-17E 41-2500 GEM of THE MOUNTAINS of the 19th BG, Java, South-West Pacific, February 1942

Delivered to Langley Field, Virginia, on 5 January 1941 and assigned to the 7th BG in Java on 19 February 1942, this aircraft's career was cut short when it was destroyed by strafing Japanese fighters at Bandoeng on 24 February 1942.

13

B-17E 41-2520 "JAP-HAPPY" of the 23rd BS/5th BG, South Pacific, 1942-43

Delivered to Ogden on 20 January 1942, this aircraft was sent to the Cheyenne, Wyoming, and Lowry, Colorado, Modification Centers before flying to Hamilton Field on 27 May 1942 and being assigned to the Seventh Air Force in Hawaii. Having survived a long tour in the South Pacific, *"JAP-HAPPY"* returned to the US on 2 September 1944 and was sold for scrap on 14 August 1945.

14

B-17E 41-2523 "GOONIE" of the 98th BS/11th BG, South Pacific, 1942-43

Delivered to Ogden on 30 January 1942 and assigned to the 98th BS/11th BG in Hawaii *"GOONIE"* was damaged by Japanese fighters on the 24 September 1942 mission to Tonolei Harbour, although pilot Lt Walter Y Lucas managed to land safely at Henderson Field. *"GOONIE"* was badly damaged again five days later whilst being flown by Lt Durbin, the bomber being intercepted by 15 Zeros whilst returning from a raid on Bougainville. Navigator S/Sgt Eber J Nealy was wounded in the head and right thigh by 20 mm cannon and 7.7-in machine gun rounds. *"GOONIE"* was credited with seven Japanese aircraft destroyed in only 15 missions, and carried a gold star on its nose denoting its participation in the Battle of Midway – all Midway veterans were so decorated. Transferred to the 5th BG, *"GOONIE"* flew missions for 38 consecutive days before being ditched off the Russell Islands on 20 March 1943 whilst being flown by 5th BG CO, Col Marion D Unruh. He and his crew were rescued.

15

B-17E 41-2525 MADAME-X of the 98th BS/11th BG, South Pacific, 1942-43

Delivered to Ogden on 25 January 1942 and then flown from Hill, prior to being sent to the Cheyenne and Lowry Modification Centers, 41-2525 left Hamilton Field for assignment to the 98th BS/11th BG in Hawaii. Later, *MADAME-X*, which was named after a pre-war movie and often flown by Lt Cope's crew, transferred to the 31st BS/5th BG and was written off at Kahili on 6 June 1943.

16

B-17E 41-2609 LOOSE-GOOSE of the 63rd BS/43rd BG, South-West Pacific, 1942-43

Delivered to Lowry Modification Center in Colorado on 8 May 1942, and then operated at Hamilton Field from 28 May to 13 July, 41-2609 was duly assigned to the 19th BG in Hawaii. It later transferred to the 43rd BG and returned to the US, arriving back at Hamilton Field on 22 July 1944. Flown to Tinker on 14 September 1944, *LOOSE-GOOSE* was sold to the Reclamation Finance Center (RFC) for scrapping on 9 February 1945.

17

B-17E 41-2621 "THE DAYLIGHT" LTD. of the 93rd BS/19th BG, Mareeba, Australia, Summer 1942

Delivered to Lowry Modification Center on 14 March and then based at Boise, Idaho from 1 April 1942, "THE DAYLIGHT" LTD. was assigned to the 93rd BS/19th BG in Hawaii on 8 July. Lt Casper crash-landed the aircraft at Mareeba on 26 August 1942 and the bomber was written off.

18

B-17E 41-2632 "CROCK O' CRAP" of the 93rd BS/ 19th BG, South-West Pacific, 1942-43

Delivered to Lowry Modification Center on 5 March and then based at Boise, Idaho, from 7 April 1942, this aircraft was assigned to the Seventh Air Force in Hawaii on 28 May. "CROCK O' CRAP" returned to the US, arriving at Hendricks on 21 December 1943. From 9 August 1945 the aircraft was at Albuquerque waiting to be scrapped.

19

B-17E 41-2656 "Chief Seattle" from the PACIFIC NORTHWEST of the 435th BS/19th BG, South-West Pacific, 1942-43

Delivered to Lowry Modification Center on 7 February 1942, and assigned to the 43rd BS/19th BG in Hawaii on 29 May, this grandiosely named aircraft was lost whilst being flown on a reconnaissance mission by Lt Cook and his crew on 19 August 1942.

20

B-17E 41-9029 FENNELL-VS-ROMMEL of the 7th BG/19th BG, South-West Pacific, 1942-43

Little is known about this Fortress other than it was delivered to MacDill Field, Florida, on 17 March 1942 and operated from West Palm Beach from 30 March. Quite who 'Fennell' was remains a mystery, and his chances of fighting 'Rommel' (German Field Marshal Erwin Rommel presumably?) in the South-West Pacific were non existent! Perhaps the artwork was added in the US when it seemed the B-17 would be heading for North Africa rather than the Pacific. 41-9029 was eventually written off on 21 November 1945.

21

B-17E 41-9093 "SPOOOOK! of the 431st BS/11th BG, South Pacific, 1942-43

Delivered to Geiger Field on 8 April 1942 and operated by the 301st BG, before moving to Lowry Modification Center on 31 May, this aircraft was assigned to the 72nd BS/5th BG in Hawaii on 7 June 1942. "SPOOOOK! returned to the US on 27 December 1943, being issued to the 2138th Base Unit (BU) at Tyndall, in Florida. Stored at Kingman from 22 October 1944, 41-9093 went to the RFC at Albuquerque on 25 June 1945 for scrapping.

22

B-17E 41-9153 TOKYO TAXI of the 394th BS/5th BG, Thirteenth Air Force, South Pacific, July 1942-July 1943

Delivered to Geiger Field on 29 April 1942 and operated by the 301st BG, this aircraft went to Lowry Modification Center on 31 May and was then assigned to the Seventh Air Force in Hawaii on 7 June 1942. TOKYO TAXI was transferred to the Thirteenth Air Force on 22 July 1942, and operated until 1943 when it was written off on 19 July in the Solomon Islands. Note the MV (air-to-surface-vessel) 'whisker brooms' search radar antennae protruding from the upper nose – two more aerials were fixed under the wings as well.

23

B-17E 41-9211 TYPHOON McGOON II of the 98th BS/11th BG, South Pacific, 1942-43

41-9211 was sent to the Cheyenne Modification Center, Wyoming, on 22 May 1942. Like TOKYO TAXI, this aircraft was also fitted with MV 'whisker brooms'. The six Japanese kill markings are for the aircraft claimed shot down on 14 November 1942 by Capt Joham's gunners when they spotted a large Japanese task force north-west of Guadalcanal. The aircraft returned to the US and was assigned to the 901st BU at Orlando on 14 December 1945. The first TYPHOON McGOON was lost on 13 September 1942.

24

B-17E 41-9227 YANKEE DOODLE JR. of the 431st BS/11th BG, South Pacific, 1942-43

Sent to the Modification Center at Cheyenne on 23 May 1942 and assigned to the 11th BG in Hawaii on 6 June 1942, this aircraft was later transferred to the 43rd BG. It was eventually written off when it crashed on take-off on 31 December 1944 while on a ferry mission to pick up liquor supplies!

25

B-17E 41-9244 HONI KUU OKOLE of the 64th BS/ 43rd BG, South-West Pacific, 1942-43

Sent to the Modification Center at Cheyenne on 29 May 1942 and assigned to the 19th BG in Hawaii on 6 August 1942, HONI KUU OKOLE (which is Hawaiian for 'Kiss My Ass') eventually transferred to the 43rd BG. It was still serving with this unit when it was shot down over Rabaul on 21 May 1943 by a Japanese nightfighter.

26

B-17F-1-BO 41-24353 CAP'N & THE KIDS of the 63rd BS/43rd BG, South-West Pacific, 1942-43

41-24353 was sent to the Modification Center at Cheyenne on 28 June 1942 and flown to Australia by Lt James T Murphy for assignment to the 63rd BS/43rd BG. One of the first F-models to reach the frontline, CAP'N & THE KIDS was usually flown by Capt Edward W Scott Jr, who was a pioneer of skip-bombing tactics. Gen George C Kenney flew in this aircraft with Capt John Van Trigt to oversee the parachute drop during the assault on Nadzab, in New Guinea, on 5 September 1943. 42-24353 flew more than 80 combat missions, the last being as a 'weather ship' for an abortive mission to Rabaul on 18 October 1943. It was credited with sinking eight Japanese ships and downing ten enemy fighters. In November 1943 CAP'N & THE KIDS was modified to armed transport configuration at the 4th Air Depot (AD) at Garbutt Field, Townsville, and was assigned to the 69th TCS/433rd TCG, 54th TCW on 23 February 1944. It was one of eight war-weary B-17s that took part in essential operations delivering weapons, ammunition and medical supplies to Momote Island during the invasion of the Admiralty Islands between 19 February-4 March 1944. The aircraft participated in further supply drops the following month during the invasion of Hollandia. In August that year CAP'N & THE KIDS was assigned to Eighth Army CO Gen Robert L Eichelberger, who renamed the B-17 Miss Em' for his wife, Emaline. Maj Charles Downer flew the aircraft from Townsville to Hollandia on 11 September 1944, and was its pilot until August 1945, during which time Miss Em' completed no fewer than 160 flights, including 63 combat missions, in 141 days. The aircraft was finally scrapped at Tacloban, Leyte, on 31 April 1946.

27

B-17F-1-BO 41-24358 Lulu Belle of the 63rd BS/43rd BG, Nadzab, New Guinea, South-West Pacific, 1942-43

Sent to the Modification Center at Cheyenne on 28 June 1942, and flown to Australia by Capt Franklin T Green for assignment to the 63rd BS/43rd BG, Lulu Belle was modified to armed transport configuration at the 4th AD at Garbutt Field. Like CAP'N & THE KIDS, it was assigned to the 69th TCS/433rd TCG in November 1943. Eventually declared war weary, Lulu Belle was stripped of its camouflage and used as a hack by Fifth Air Force HQ staffers at Nadzab, New Guinea, until was scrapped in Manila on 13 September 1945.

28

B-17F-1-BO 41-24384 of the 63rd BS/43rd BG, Sumac, South Pacific, Summer 1942.

Sent to the Modification Center at Cheyenne on 26 June 1942, this aircraft departed Hamilton Field on 28 July and was flown to Australia by Capt James A Barnett's crew. It flew combat indoctrination missions in the 19th BG and was later flown by Maj Felix Hardison on the Rabaul mission on 29 August 1942. The aircraft was transferred to the 63rd BS/43rd BG and flown by Lt James T Murphy and crew until February 1943, when it was modified for long-range reconnaissance missions. On 2 March 1943, during the prelude to the Battle of the Bismarck Sea, Lt Herbert Derr flew a 'shadow recon' mission of more than 11 hours in 41-24384, reporting the movement of the Japanese convoy and giving weather reports to V Bomber Command. On 26 March 1943 the Fortress disappeared without trace whilst on a long range reconnaissance flight with Brig Gen Howard Ramey, newly-appointed CO of V Bomber Command, aboard.

29

B-17F-5-BO 41-24403 The Old Man of the 65th BS/43rd BG (formerly Blitz Buggy of the 30th BS/19th BG), South-West Pacific, 1942-43

Delivered on 26 June 1942 and sent to the Modification Center at Cheyenne on 30 June, this aircraft reached the 30th BS/19th BG at Mareeba on 21 August 1942. Named Blitz Buggy, the bomber starting operating from Port Moresby on 15 September. Late in 1942 it was reassigned to the 65th BS/43rd BG and flown regularly by Lt Glen Lewis and his crew. In January 1943, with the aircraft having been renamed The Old Man and adorned with a cheerful 'Uncle Sam', 41-24403 was transferred to the 63rd BS when the 65th BS began converting to the B-24. The Old Man flew a number of missions during July-August 1943 and flew its very last combat sortie on 18 August, when Lt William Crawford piloted the B-17 on a strike against Wewak. The Old Man then became a transport hack and was used by Gen Ennis Whitehead, commander of Advon, Fifth Air Force. The radio compartment was fitted out to carry two passengers, with two seats facing each other on the starboard side, and aft of the radio room bulkhead was a separate compartment with a bed. All of the armament except the ball turret was retained – this was removed, and a 24-volt refrigerator installed in its place! The Old Man was scrapped in the Philippines after July 1948.

30

B-17F-10-BO 41-24446 JEZABEL of the 42nd BS/11th BG, South Pacific, 1942-43

Delivered to the USAAF on 26 June 1942 and to the Modification Center at Cheyenne on 10 July, this aircraft was assigned to Capt Edward Steedman and his crew in Hawaii and ordered to Australia, via Christmas Island, Canton and Fiji. Steedman took off from Fiji at 0200 hrs on 15 August 1942 for the 11-hour flight to Brisbane, but en route the crew were told to land in New Caledonia, where the aircraft was assigned to the 42nd BS/11th BG on 30 August. On 15 September JEZABEL was transferred to the 431st BS. It eventually returned to the US on 8 November 1944.

31

B-17F-10-BO 41-24448 TAXPAYER'S PRIDE of the 64th BS/43rd BG, Fifth Air Force, Sumac, South-West Pacific, September 1942-June 1943

In August 1942 West Point graduate Capt Jay P Rousek and crew, who had flown B-17B/Ds in the 74th BG in Panama, were flown to Sacramento SAD to pick up 41-24448. Sgt Frank Hohmann, flight engineer, recalls;

'The whole crew was assembled on a platform that had been moved into place just for the occasion. A large crowd of people that worked there had subscribed to the cost of the aeroplane. They were shouting, "Name the plane!" We put our heads together and Rousek came up with the name, TAXPAYER'S PRIDE. The crowd went wild and the painter painted this name on the nose.'

On 10 August the Rousek crew left for Hickam Field, a flight of 13 hrs 30 min, then off again on the morning of 12 August for Christmas Island, a 7 hr 45 min flight. On the morning of the 13th the crew flew to Canton, a British Short Sunderland flying boat station. Next morning they took-off again for Fiji. They were within ten miles of the halfway point when they had a runaway propeller on the No 2 engine, which refused to feather, so they turned around and flew back to Canton with the prop slowly turning – a six-hour flight for nothing. No suitable replacement parts were forthcoming from the Hawaiian Air Depot, so Frank Hohmann improvised using a small governor and a plumber's pipe fitting to connect the prop feathering line. *TAXPAYER'S PRIDE* took off again for Fiji on 20 August. Hohmann adds;

'No problems – 6 hrs 50 min. On 22 August we flew to New Caledonia in 4 hrs 50 min. When we got ready to land the co-pilot, Vern Strawser, said he wanted to make the landing. Jay said okay and Vern brought the aeroplane around to line up with the runway and started to let down. Just before touch-down a wild cross-wind took him to the right off the runway, where our outboard engine propeller caught the top of a sign saying *WELCOME TO NEW CALEDONIA* and tore it to pieces! Vern spent the rest of the evening explaining to the base commander how he didn't see the sign. *TAXPAYER'S PRIDE* arrived at Amberley Field, Ipswich, near Brisbane, on 23 August. We took off two days later for Mareeba, which would be our home-away-from-home for the next six months. We were assigned to the 28th BS of the 19th BG. We flew our first mission in *Taxpayer's Pride* on 29 August 1942 – a 2 hr 30 min trip over the Coral Sea, along the south coast of New Guinea. Engine trouble cut the flight short. Because we didn't rule the seas at that time, the mission turned out to be a combat one. On 30 August we took off for a recon of the eastern end of New Guinea – mainly the Milne Bay area – to check if the Japs had any intentions of another run at landing at Port Moresby. We landed there to get orders. No targets, so we were sent back to Mareeba. The Japs were coming over the Owen Stanley Range every night to try to hit something and we didn't have too many aeroplanes that could fly due to a shortage of spare parts. Then they took *TAXPAYER'S PRIDE* away from us because it was a new aeroplane, and a recon squadron needed it.'

On 26 June 1943 *TAXPAYER'S PRIDE*, now in the 64th BS/43rd BG, was shot down by a Japanese nightfighter while returning from a mission to Rabaul. The bomber's tail gunner Sgt Joel Griffin was the only survivor from Lt Donald McEachran's crew.

32

B-17F-10-BO 41-24454 *GEORGIA PEACH* of the 63rd BS/43rd BG, South-West Pacific, July 1942-June 1943

Delivered on 10 July 1942 and sent to the Modification Center at Cheyenne on 13 July, this aircraft was assigned to the 28th BS/19th BG in Australia. *GEORGIA PEACH* later transferred to the 65th BS/43rd BG and was caught in searchlights over Rabaul on 13 June 1943 and shot down by a Japanese Navy J1N1 *Irving* nightfighter of the 251st *Kokutai*. Of Lt John Woodward's crew who were aboard the B-17, only bombardier Lt Jack Wisener and navigator Lt Philip Bek survived. Wisener became a PoW but the Japanese killed Bek.

33

B-17F-10-BO 41-24455 *OLD BALDY* of the 63rd BS/43rd BG, Sumac, South Pacific, Summer 1942-November 1943

Sent to the Modification Center at Cheyenne on 9 July 1942 and then flown to Australia by Lt James G DeWolf, 41-24455 was assigned to the 63rd BS/ 43rd BG. Once in-theatre, the bomber's first pilot was Jim Dieffenderfer, who recalls;

'When we were told we could put names on our aircraft, I talked to my crew and we decided to let the groundcrew chief choose the name. We figured he would do an outstanding job if he was maintaining "his" aircraft. Al Falk from New Jersey chose the name, and he always had it ready for missions.'

OLD BALDY returned to the US on 12 November 1943 and was used for training by the 398th BG at Rapid City, South Dakota, and at Biggs Field, Texas, before being written off on 3 September 1944.

34

B-17F-10-BO 41-24457 *The AZTEC'S CURSE* of the 26th BS/11th BG and 31st BS/5th BG, South Pacific, 1942-43

41-24457 was delivered on 10 July 1942 and sent to the Cheyenne and Lowry Modification Centers, before being assigned to the 26th BS/11th BG on 24 August 1942. When the 11th BG moved back to Hawaii in February 1943, the Fortress was transferred to the 31st BS/5th BG where, on 23 April, it suffered a brake failure on landing and Capt Leon Rockwell ground-looped the aircraft. Undamaged in the incident, an inattentive ground tug then arrived and knocked off the tail guns, which resulted in the B-17 having to be salvaged a few days later!

35

B-17F-10-BO 41-24458 *San Antonio Rose* of the 19th BG and 64th BS/43rd BG, South-West Pacific, 1942-43

This aircraft was delivered on 8 July 1942 and sent to the Cheyenne, Wyoming and Lowry Modification Centers, before being assigned to the 19th BG and, finally, the 64th BS/43rd BG. *San Antonio Rose* and Maj Allen Lindberg's crew from the 64th BS/43rd BG were shot down after bombing Rabaul Harbour on 5 January 1943, with none of its crew surviving. Amongst the casualties was V Bomber Command CO, Brig Gen Kenneth N Walker.

36

B-17F-20-BO 41-24521 *BLACK JACK/The JOKER'S WILD* of the 63rd BS/43rd BG, South-West Pacific, 1943

Delivered to Lowry Modification Center on 29 July 1942, this aircraft was based at Hamilton from 31 August that year before being assigned to the 63rd BS/43rd BG, where this Fortress, and its pilot, Capt Ken McCullar, became legendary. In September 1942 McCullar, a flamboyant gambler and a totally fearless and aggressive pilot, noted the last two digits of its serial number (41-24521) and had the name and two playing cards (a 'Jack' and an 'ace') painted on the nose by Sgt Ernie Vandal. McCullar had Sgt Tony DeAngelis and his groundcrew install a fixed 0.50-cal machine gun in the nose, with a firing button on the pilot's control wheel, so that he could blast away at enemy ships and help deter head-on attacks by fighters. On the night of 24 November 1942 McCullar sank the Japanese destroyer *Hayashio* in the Huon Gulf after making five very low bombing runs in *BLACK JACK*. Heavily damaged, the bomber was out of action for two months. During that time McCullar's co-pilot, Lt Harry Staley, took over the Fortress, and he had Sgt Vandal paint the words *The JOKER'S WILD*, as well as a devil's playing card, on the port side of the forward fuselage. Staley's crew flew five missions in 41-24521 before the Fortress was badly shot up over Rabaul on 14 February 1943. They went on to complete their missions in other aircraft. *BLACK JACK/The JOKER'S WILD* returned to combat status in April 1943, after which it had become something of a lucky ship, being flown by 13 different pilots in the 63rd BS in 14 missions. However, on 11 July 1943, Lt Ralph De Loach's crew failed to return from the mission to Vunakanau airfield, on Rabaul, in 41-24521. The pilot had put the bomber down in deep water off Bogaboga village in the Milne Bay province of New Guinea, and the crew was subsequently rescued.

37

B-17F-20-BO 41-24537 *Talisman* of the 63rd BS/43rd BG, New Guinea, South-West Pacific, 1943

Delivered on 30 July 1942 and sent to the Modification Center at Cheyenne on 2 August, this aircraft was flown from Hamilton Field to Australia by Lt William E O'Brien, the bomber being assigned to the 63rd BS/43rd BG upon its arrival. On 5 September 1943 Col Harry Hawthorne, CO of the 43rd BG, flew *Talisman* with Gen Howard Ramey of V Bomber Command in the co-pilot's seat and Gen Douglas MacArthur 'back aft' to observe the parachute drop during the invasion on Nadzab, in New Guinea. Its luck held, and when the bomber was declared war-weary *Talisman* returned to the US. While shooting some landings at Jackson Field, Florida, on 24 April 1943, Lt James H Powell crashed the aircraft, which was repaired and renamed *USASOS War-Horse.* It was then issued to Maj Gen James L Frink, CO of Services of Supply, South-West Pacific, who used

it as a hack transport. The aircraft was duly salvaged on 9 September 1945 at Tacloban, Leyte.

38

B-17F-25-BO 41-24554 *The MUSTANG* of the 63rd BS/43rd BG, South-West Pacific, October 1942 to 1943

Delivered on 5 August 1942 and sent to Lowry Modification Center on 7 August, this aircraft was based at Hamilton Field from 6 October 1942, and was assigned to the 403rd BS/43rd BG on 17 October 1942. Later, *The MUSTANG* transferred to the 63rd BS. On 5 September 1943 Gen Richard Sutherland, MacArthur's chief of staff, was aboard *The MUSTANG* as part of Gen Kenney's 'brass hat's flight' that was sortied to oversee the parachute drop during the invasion on Nadzab, in New Guinea. 41-24554 returned to the US on 2 December 1943 and was used for training at Rapid City by the 398th BG and at Walker Field, Kansas. The Fortress ended its days, like so many others, at RFC Albuquerque sometime after being sold for scrap on 25 June 1945.

39

B-17F-25-BO 41-24574 *TUFFY* of the 403rd BS/43rd BG, South-West Pacific, November 1942 to 1943

Delivered on 11 August 1942 and sent to Cheyenne Modification Center on 12 August, 41-24574 was based at Hamilton from 9 November and assigned to the 43rd BG five days later. During the Battle of the Bismarck Sea, on 2 March 1943, Maj Ed Scott, pilot of *TUFFY,* dropped two bombs on a large destroyer from 7000 ft, which set the vessel on fire. He then dived the B-17, levelled out at 50 ft and his gunners, incensed at the shooting of a crew helpless in their parachutes after baling out that morning, blasted away at every survivor in sight. *TUFFY* served in both the 63rd and 403rd BSs, flying its last combat mission on 16 October 1943, and returned to the US on 3 November. Used in Rapid City for training by the 398th BG, the bomber was scrapped at RFC Altus after 30 August 1945.

Back cover

B-17F-25-BO 41-24552 *LISTEN HERE. TOJO!* of the 65th BS/43rd BG, Sumac, South-West Pacific, 1942-43

This bomber was delivered on 4 August 1942 and assigned to the 403rd BS/43rd BG on 5 November 1942. On 15 September 1943 *LISTEN HERE. TOJO!* and Lt Howard G Eberley's crew were last seen peeling off to the left as the formation entered a large thunderhead whilst returning to Port Moresby after a bombing mission. Attempts to reach the crew by radio went unanswered, and it was assumed the B-17 had flown into a cloud-covered mountain peak. This was the last B-17 to be lost in combat operations in the south-west Pacific. In 1992 the wreckage of *LISTEN HERE. TOJO!* was found at 8900 ft on a mountain 13 miles south-west of Lae, New Guinea. In 1993 the remains of the crew were recovered and returned to the US.

BIBLIOGRAPHY

Beck, Alfred M (chief editor). *With Courage – The US Army Air Forces of World War 2.* Air Force History & Museums Program, 1994

Bendiner, Elmer. *Fall of the Fortresses.* Putnam, 1980

Birdsall, Steve. *The B-17 Flying Fortress.* Morgan 1965

Birdsall, Steve. *Pride of Seattle – The Story of the first 300 B-17Fs.* Squadron Signal, 1998

Birdsall, Steve. *Fighting Colors – B-17 Flying Fortress.* Squadron Signal, 1986

Birdsall, Steve. *Hell's Angels B-17 Combat Markings.* Grenadier Books, 1969

Birdsall, Steve. *Flying Buccaneers; The Illustrated Story of Kenney's Fifth Air Force.* David & Charles, 1978

Birdsall, Steve & Freeman, Roger A. *Claims to Fame – The B-17 Flying Fortress.* Arms & Armour, 1994

Birdsall, Steve. *Black Jack's last Mission,* Warbirds Worldwide Special Edition

Bowers, Peter M. *Boeing Aircraft Since 1916.* Putnam, 1966

Bowers Peter M. *Fortress in The Sky.* Sentry, 1976

Bowman, M W. *Flying To Glory.* PSL, 1992

Bowman, M W. *Boeing B-17 Flying Fortress.* Crowood, 1998

Byrd, Martha, (Preston Bryant, editor). *Kenneth N Walker – Airpower's Untempered Crusader.* Air University Press, 1997

Caidin, Martin. *Flying Forts – the B-17 in World War 2.* Ballantine, 1968

Collison, Thomas. *Flying Fortress – The Story of the Boeing Bomber.* Scribner, 1943

Davis, Larry. *B-17 In Action.* Squadron/Signal, 1984

Edmonds, Walter D. *They Fought with What They Had.* Washington Center for Air Force History, 1993

Ethell, Jeffrey L and Simonsen, Clarence. *The History of Aircraft NOSE ART - World War 1 to Today.* Motorbooks, 1991

Freeman, Roger A. *B-17 Fortress At War.* Ian Allan Ltd, 1977

Hess, William. *B-17 Flying Fortress.* Ballantine, 1974

Jablonski, Edward. *Flying Fortress.* Doubleday, 1965

Johnsen, Fred. *Winged Majesty.* PNAHF, 1980

Lloyd, Alwyn T and Moore, Terry D. *B-17 Flying Fortress in detail & scale.* Aero Publishers Inc

McDowell, Ernest R. *Flying Fortress in Action.* Squadron Signal, 1987

McDowell, Ernest R. *Flying Fortress – The Boeing B-17.* Squadron/Signal, 1987

Murphy, James T and Feuer, A B. *'Skip Bombing'.* Praeger, July 1993

Nichols, Paul. *My Lucky Dice.* self-published

Salecker, Gene Eric. *Fortress against the Sun – the B-17 Flying Fortress in the Pacific.* Schiffer, February 2001

Scutts, Jerry. *B-17 Flying Fortress.* PSL, 1982

Siefring, T A. *US Army Air Force in World War 2.* Chartwell, 1977

Thompson, Charles D. *The Boeing B-17E and F Flying Fortress.* Profile, 1966

Walker, Howell. *American Bombers Attacking from Australia.* National Geographic Magazine, 1943

Wilmmott H P. *B-17 Flying Fortress.* Chartwell, 1980

Websites
www.pacificghosts.com
www.aerothentic.com_

INDEX

References to illustrations are shown in **bold**. Plates are shown with page and caption locators in brackets.